THE
STORY
of
COLOUR

THE
STORY
of
COLOUR

AN EXPLORATION OF THE HIDDEN
MESSAGES OF THE SPECTRUM

GAVIN EVANS

Michael O'Mara Books Limited

First published in Great Britain in 2017 by
Michael O'Mara Books Limited
9 Lion Yard
Tremadoc Road
London SW4 7NQ

A CIP catalogue record for this book is available from the
British Library.

Papers used by Michael O'Mara Books Limited are natural,
recyclable products made from wood grown in sustainable
forests. The manufacturing processes conform to the
environmental regulations of the country of origin.

ISBN: 978-1-78243-690-4 in hardback print format
ISBN: 978-1-78243-691-1 in ebook format

1 3 5 7 9 10 8 6 4 2

Follow us on Twitter @OMaraBooks
www.mombooks.com

Cover design and interior page design by Ana Bjezancevic
Designed and typeset by ROCKJAW Creative

Printed and bound in China

To my daughters Tessa and Caitlin: it would be an awful cliché to say you put colour in my life, but I'll say it anyway.

CONTENTS

INTRODUCTION

I f pupils were concentrating at school they might have learnt the mnemonic 'Roy G Biv', one way of teaching children the usual order of colours of the rainbow – red, orange, yellow, green, blue, indigo, violet – just as some British children learn the alternative 'Richard of York gave battle in vain'. In India pupils learn VIBGYOR, which is the reverse order of Roy G Biv. Either way round, no purple and most definitely no pink.

And yet, are red, orange, yellow, green, blue, indigo and violet really the 'correct' colours of the rainbow? Well, yes, and one can add to the list or subtract, as long as one doesn't throw in grey or gold or brown, or pink, for that matter. It all depends on where one lives, or when one lived, because the received colours of the rainbow have changed according to culture and over time.

Let us go back to the man who invented what became Roy G Biv: perhaps the most remarkable scientist of them all, Isaac Newton. Along with his discoveries on the laws of planetary motion and of gravity, and his co-discovery of calculus and his huge contribution to developing the scientific method, he was obsessed with light and colour. This prompted one of his most famous experiments (in his rooms, during the Great Plague, when the university was closed). Using a partition board with a pinhole in it and a glass prism, he observed how white light can be broken into the colours of the rainbow.

As Newton explained it: 'In a very dark chamber, at a round hole, about one-third part of an inch broad, made in the shut of a window, I placed a glass prism, whereby the beam of the sun's light, which came in that hole, might be refracted upwards toward the opposite wall the chamber, and there form a coloured image of the sun.'

He showed that white light is the combination of the full colour spectrum. In his book *Opticks* (1704), he explained how these colours comprise light rays that bend, or refract, at different angles when passing through a prism, so the colours separate. The ray that bends the most is violet, with the shortest wavelength, and the least is red, with the longest wavelength. In the middle is green. Crucially, he reversed the experiment too, demonstrating that the spectrum of colours can be reassembled into white light.

A century on, in a book titled *Theory of Colour*, the great German thinker Johann von Goethe described Newton's idea that white light was a combination of all the colours as 'an absurdity' and he moaned about people parroting Newton's idea 'in opposition to the evidence of their senses'. What Newton understood, and Goethe failed to grasp, was the difference between the colours of the paintbox and those of light. Mix the pigments of the artist's palette together and one gets a very dirty grey-brown. But when considering light, it all changes. Spin a colour wheel fast enough and it will appear white.

Right: Sir Isaac Newton examining the nature of light with the aid of a prism. This allowed him to see that white light is comprised of multiple colours, what we now call the colours of the spectrum.

There are other differences, too. In the paintbox the primary colours are red, blue and yellow, with all others a combination of these. With light, the primary colours are green, blue and red. Mix all three equally and one gets white. Mix varying ratios of these and one can get any other colour in the rainbow. Every picture or illustration we see on our televisions or our laptops or smartphones is the product of tiny green, blue and red dots.

Despite his scientific and mathematical genius, Newton was very much a man of his time, one whom John Maynard Keynes called 'the last of the magicians'. When taking breaks from advancing science and mathematics, and from hanging counterfeiters and excoriating his scientific rivals, Newton spent his time studying the Holy Trinity, the occult and searching for the philosopher's stone. He had a mystical fondness for the supposedly magical properties of the number seven, which he also saw as the prime number of nature (the seven notes of the Western musical scale, the seven planets of the solar system, and so on).

After some prevarication, Newton opted for seven colours of the rainbow, rather than the previous five or six (the colours he added were orange and indigo). Really, there are no pure colours in a rainbow, as such, for they all blend into one continuous spectrum. We might see seven but in reality there is not a delineated gradient, which means the boundaries are blurred and the divisions arbitrary. Interestingly, the colour orange did not exist in Europe until the orange fruit was introduced. Prior to its introduction, 'orange' objects were described as gold or golden, which is why we have goldfish instead of orangefish. In fact, tomatoes were originally called golden apples, too.

When we see the full range of visible light waves together, our eyes and our brains say 'white' but when some of those wavelengths are missing we see them as colours. More accurately, objects absorb different parts of the white light spectrum, so we see those parts that are reflected. But the colours the human eye chooses to see and how it chooses to see them varies from one culture to another and even from one individual to another.

In English indigo is really another word for dark blue and violet is often used as an alternative word for purple. Newton's blue could also be called turquoise, and so on. We all see the same range of colours when we look at the rainbow, but how we identify them differs. According to the philosopher Xenophon, the Ancient Greeks identified only three colours in the rainbow – red, yellow and purple. Ancient Arab tradition also agreed on three – but they used red, yellow and green.

Part of our colour perception relates to the genes we happen to inherit individually. Yet rather more important are cultural differences, which have been influenced by the way our societies have used colour over time – and the number of colours in our cultural palette has expanded as we have found new ways of capturing the hues of nature in paints, dyes, tints and pigments, and in how we use colours and patterns to adorn ourselves, our homes, our places of work and our possessions.

Language plays a significant role. The colours we see and use find their way into our languages, and the way we see is influenced by language – by the words we use to describe objects. Take blue and green. To Western eyes these are very clearly different colours – alongside each other on the colour wheel, but distinct, as blue is a pure or primary colour and green is a mixed or secondary. However, as we shall see in the chapter on blue, several modern and ancient languages have just one word for both. To some that may seem odd. Yet in English the word blue covers both light blue and dark blue, whereas in Russian these colours are as distinct as pink and red. While all shades of green are described as 'green' in English, in Korean there are different words for two shades of green – one more yellowish than the other.

MEN, WOMEN AND COLOUR-BLINDNESS

Some people are naturally better at distinguishing colours than others. About 4.5 per cent of Western populations are defined as 'colour-blind'. This does not mean that they see in black and white, or monochrome; it means that they lack either red or green retinal cone cells, so they can't tell the difference between red and green, such as on traffic lights. In some cases, they have difficulty distinguishing blue and yellow. Between population groups there are no differences in the genes that relate to mental abilities, but there can be slight differences in the genes that govern physical attributes. One of these relates to the ability to see colour. Among the Pingelap tribe, in Micronesia, it has been estimated that 10 per cent of the population is colour-blind – more than double the international average.

Below: Two colour perception tests, known as 'Ishihara' tests, for red-green colour deficiencies.

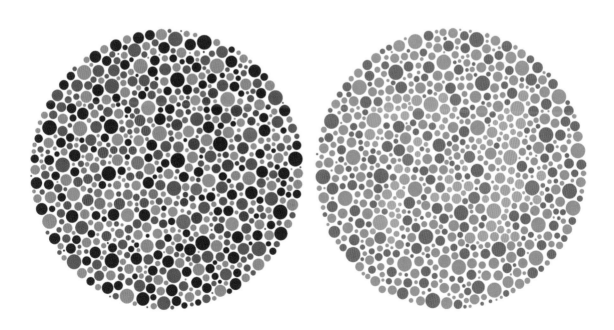

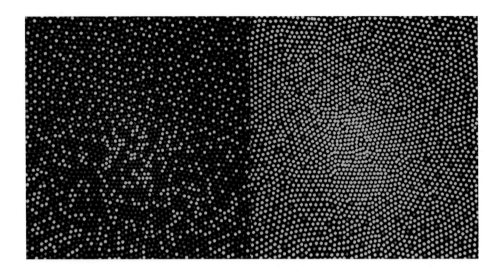

In Britain, 8 per cent of men are colour-blind but only 0.5 per cent of women. In addition, more women than men are 'tetrachromatic', meaning they have an extra retinal cone, making them super-sensitive to colour distinction.

The normal eye is trichromatic: it has three types of cones that detect colour from three parts of the spectrum. One study found that between 2 and 3 per cent of women had inherited this heightened colour perception. Curiously, colour-blind boys have higher odds of having tetrachromatic mothers and daughters, due to dominant and recessive gene combinations.

Above: Illustration of the distribution of cone cells in the part of the human eye used for detailed perception; in a person with normal colour vision (left) and a colour-blind retina (right).

RODS, CONES AND ANIMAL EYES

Not all animals are colour-blind. In fact, several see better than humans in terms of distance and colour range. Many insects can see ultraviolet colour (helping them to find flowers to feed from), while some snakes can detect infrared (helping them detect heat from their mammal prey). Apes have similar colour perception to humans, but most other mammals fall into the same category as colour-blind people (dogs and cats, for example), and some (such as bats and many herbivores) see no colour at all, only shades of grey – they are monochromatic.

What it comes down to is the animal's photoreceptors in the retina of the eye, which consist of rods and cones. Light enters the retina before being interpreted by the rods and cones, which send messages to the primary visual cortex within the brain, prompting the perception of colour and tones. Cones are responsible for colour perception, while rods are responsible for detecting contrast, so that we can sense movement in low-light conditions. The pupil naturally adjusts in size to optimize these perceptions according to light levels.

LIGHT AND COLOUR

How we see colour is affected by the way light reflects from the surfaces of objects, so this can vary. When we look at our living room, we might say the couch is green, the curtains are red, the floor is brown and the armchair is blue. These appear to be their colours, but if we change the lighting then the colours change too; switch off the light and red, brown and blue effectively become shades of grey, due to the low light levels.

If we move outside into the bright midday sunlight, we'll see the full range of colours detectable to the human eye, but as the sun goes down, light levels drop and the atmosphere filters the colours, reducing the range of colour rays. In the 1890s the French impressionist Claude Monet (1840–1926) illustrated this by painting at least thirty pictures of Rouen Cathedral at different times of the day and year, with the colours changing accordingly.

Artificial light exposes our eyes to a narrower colour range than bright sunlight, depending on the kind of light bulb used.

Opposite: Monet's versions of Rouen Cathedral in different lights. See how the colours change at different times of the day and year.

For example, fluorescent light highlights cooler colours like blue and green, while incandescent bulbs pick out warm colours like red, orange and yellow. This is most dramatically illustrated by stage lighting. For example, a blue filter will turn blue into a blue-green colour and will turn yellow into black.

THE PROPERTIES OF COLOUR

We can consider colour from different angles:

- **Luminosity**: This concerns lightness and darkness and is best illustrated through black and white photographs. A black surface would have no luminosity; a white surface would have maximum luminosity. We also talk of a *shade of colour*, if it contains black, and a *tint* of a colour, if it contains white.
- **Hue:** This term, commonly used by graphic designers, relates to their wavelengths. We shift from one hue to another as their wavelengths change (on the one end of the spectrum violet is in the 390-431 nm range; on the other end, red is in the 658-780 nm range). We call a sunset orange because the light waves bouncing off its molecules are in the 600-658 nm range.
- **Saturation:** Artists and graphic designers note that some colours *appear* 'purer' than others because they have less of their surrounding colours within them – also known as a colour's 'saturation'. This can be influenced by the eye of the viewer. What, for some cultures is pure blue, for other cultures is a muted shade of green.
- **Temperature:** Half of the colours in the spectrum can be defined as 'cool' and the other half as 'warm'. This relates to their cultural associations. Red, yellow and orange – the colours of the sun and fire – are perceived as warm, while blue and green – the colours of sky, sea and leaves – are perceived as cool. But some colours fall somewhere between, such as purple and maroon.

THE MYSTERY DRESS: BLUE AND BLACK OR WHITE AND GOLD?

In 2015 a single image polarized opinion on social media. It featured a bodycon dress that appeared to be blue with a black lace fringe to some people, but white with a gold lace fringe to other people. What was going on?

Our brains interpret the light entering the lenses of our eyes, and this is influenced by light in the space we are in, the saturation of colours, the surrounding colours and the clarity of the image. The image of the dress serves to illustrate this. It had little surrounding colour context and it was slightly muted, so people's brains were required to guess. Most people's brains saw the dress as being swathed in light and therefore darkened the colours to see it as blue and black (the 'correct' interpretation, as it turns out). But some brains saw it as being shadowed and therefore compensated by lightening it – and ended up seeing white and gold. Some people can switch from one perception to the other, depending on the light in the room.

USING COLOUR IN ART

Lara Harwood, a London-based artist and illustrator, whose abstract and figurative work is known for its vivid use of colour, reveals how she is influenced by the cultural connotations of colours as she works. She consciously embraces the subtext of their meanings and believes these change when she combines them.

'When I think about the colours I intend to use in my work, I ask myself what they mean to me, and what they represent for others. Red is bold, happy, dramatic and dangerous; blue is inevitably sad, but also has a richness and light to it – if you have a lighter blue it can be the source of light for a darker blue and lots of blues together can be gorgeous; yellow is such a bright, happy, uplifting colour, but you have to be careful because it can disappear alongside white; orange is also happy and uplifting and it can hold its own as a strong base colour; purple has a very wide range. I love its moodiness and it goes well with most other colours; I use pink a great deal because it is soft and gently happy. Green is obviously such a natural colour but I don't want to use it in that way, as in, 'here's a green tree'. Brown needs brighter colours around it. Black goes with everything but it can have a heavy, flattening effect. Grey, on the other hand, does a wonderful job in showing off other colours. But when thinking about the meaning of colour in art, it is all about the combination of colours and the impact they have on each other.'

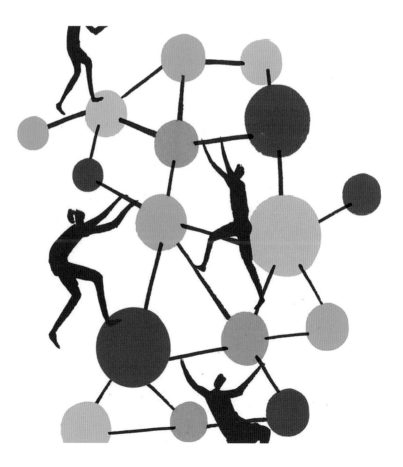

Right: Lara Harwood's illustration for the HHMI Annual Report, 2008, shows off her use off colour in her work.

RED

A GROUP OF FISHERMEN on the west coast of South Africa's Cape Province were busy in their workshop. Their aim was to make paint and they went about it with traditional knowledge and skill, carefully blending red ochre (iron oxide) with fat extracted from bone marrow to create a paint compound that was mixed in shell paint pots using bone spatulas.

We can't be sure exactly what they did with their red paint – whether it was daubed on their bodies, their tools and weapons or on the cave walls, because they were making their paint 100,000 years ago. Since then erosion has removed the evidence, but their tool kit and the residues of their red paint remain, and so do their red-stained beads, which show that, at least since that time, humans have had the ability to express and adorn themselves using colour.

THE BEGINNINGS OF EXPRESSION

Perhaps an even more remarkable discovery from the same cave, Blombos, is the oldest known example of symbolic art – some 30,000 years before anything comparable emerged in Europe: two red ochre plaques carved with triangles, diamond-shapes and lines. They have been dated to 75,000 years ago. Again, we don't know for certain what these engravings meant but finds at other coastal caves in the area have shown that symbols like these were widely used at the time, perhaps to keep a record of something. Murals from later cave dwellers in Southern Africa, Namibia, Europe, the Middle East, Australia and parts of Asia show that red was the colour of choice, as only yellow and black were also available. Images of red animals, red hands and red people have all been recorded. In the Bomvu Ridge area of Swaziland, archaeologists have found 40,000-year-old mines used to dig out red and yellow ochre, thought to be used for body painting.

Above: It may look nondescript, but this red ochre plaque excavated from the Blombos Cave in South Africa is 75,000 years old and is the oldest known piece of artwork created by human hands.

When the modern human brain evolved, at least 100,000 years ago, people started adorning themselves and expressing their thoughts symbolically and artistically. Perhaps not surprisingly, red was the first colour that all cultures shared. In the Hebrew tradition, the first man was moulded from red earth, i.e. earthenware clay. The root of the Hebrew word for Adam actually means 'red' and it is also related to the word 'dam', which means 'blood', so A-dam means 'of blood'.

To take another example, when the first white colonists sailed into North America they dubbed the native people they encountered as 'Red Indians'. This wasn't due to their natural skin colour but rather the red ochre paste they used to daub their bodies and faces. It was war paint, but might also have been used to repel insects in the summer, or to insulate bare faces in the winter, and to ward off evil spirits.

Right: These ancient cave paintings from Argentina served as an early form of communication, and show how man has desired to record his own existence for thousands of years.

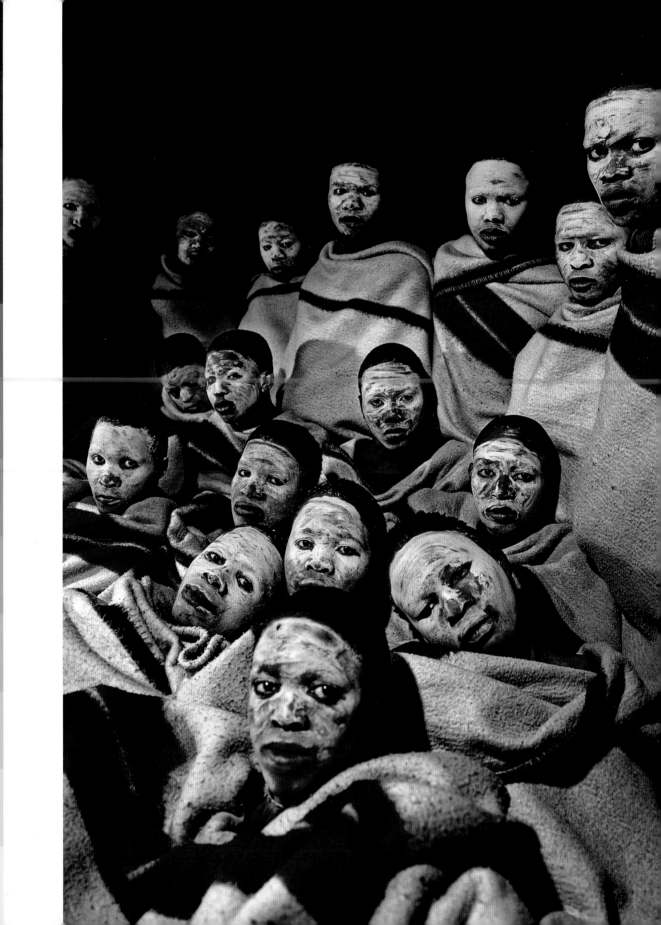

BIRTH, DEATH, FIRE AND FERTILITY

The appeal of red and its presence in prehistoric art and adornments is not just a product of prehistory and availability. In every continent it seems to have been the first colour (other than black and white) to have been named. It is an elemental shade, the colour of heat and fire. It is also the colour of autumn, due to the colour of changing leaves, the colour of rust (iron oxide) and of the red planet Mars, which is called red due to an abundance of iron oxide.

Red's early appeal had a lot to do with nature – as well as availability. But more than all this, red is the colour of blood – the medium of life, of birth, of the death thrusts of battle and of menstruation. It evokes strength, virility and fertility. In 1850, Alfred Tennyson first referred to nature as 'red in tooth and claw' – and the phrase stuck as a maxim for the bloody violence of the natural world. Blood is also alluded to in the names and symbols of the Red Cross and Red Crescent, the red representing the healing of bleeding wounds. In several languages the name of the colour is drawn from the name for blood.

Blood–birth–death–fertility symbolism appears in most cultural traditions. Young men of the Xhosa tribe in South Africa, having undergone ritual circumcision as part of their passage into manhood, are covered in red-striped blankets as they heal from the procedure, after which they are accepted by the Xhosa as men. In Zambia, Ndembu girls are handed a baby chicken covered with red ochre as a symbol of their entry to the world of menstruation, sexual intercourse and motherhood. This is washed away when they have sex for the first time and the red water is then used to encourage fertility and childbirth. During the Ancient Chinese Han dynasty (206 BC to AD 220) women in the emperor's harem placed a red mark on their foreheads to signal when they were menstruating.

In parts of northern India fathers present their daughters with red 'blood saris' on their wedding day – the red symbolizing sexual power. A bride's hair parting is also painted red, as are the soles of her feet, and she wears a red bindi on her forehead and has red henna hands. If she pre-deceases her husband, then her funeral shroud is also red. Red features prominently in the Indian and Nepalese Hindu spring festivals of *Holi*, also known as the Festival of Colour. This love feast starts with dancing and singing around a bonfire that represents the burning of the devil and the victory of good over evil. In the morning people eat, drink, play and chase each other, throwing coloured powder and spraying each other with water guns and balloons filled with tinted water – including red ochre. Today it is all about uninhibited fun, but it was originally a festival aimed at encouraging sexual activity and boosting the harvest. The red ochre was said to stimulate fertility.

Previous page: Boys of the Xhosa tribe are wrapped in red-striped blankets as they make the passage into manhood.

Above: Newlyweds, wearing traditional Han costumes, attend a group wedding ceremony in China.

Left: Revellers are covered in coloured powder and water as they celebrate *Holi*, the Festival of Colour.

The Chinese also elevate red in their colour system, which recognizes five standard colours that correspond with the five elements of traditional Chinese thought: red = fire; black = water; white = metal; yellow = earth; blue/green = wood.

Red is also the colour of celebration, seen everywhere during Chinese New Year. This is because it symbolizes joy, as well as vitality and fertility, and it is the colour of the pomegranate, which is viewed as a revitalizing fruit whose many seeds represent a rich line of descent. Red envelopes are used to offer gifts of money, given on holidays or celebrations, because red symbolizes good luck.

Red has also been thought to hold protective properties. Red clothes were worn in Ancient Roman pagan rituals as protection from evil – and from measles. In New Zealand, Maori warriors would paint their bodies with red ochre to protect them in combat. In several parts of the world, baby clothes are still decorated with red to keep babies from harm. In parts of China, babies have a red mark painted on their foreheads to protect them against evil spirits, and timid children have little red sacks attached to their clothes to give them the courage to withstand evil visions. Chinese brides, as well as their families and guests, wear red to ward off evil.

Red is additionally used to welcome one-month-old Chinese babies into the world – with eggs died in ochre. It also features in some Chinese courting rituals. In the mountainous parts of south China, the Miao people celebrate the Flower Mountain Festival, where children dance around a pole with long red streamers.

The older girls wear red woollen bonnets. In the Sisters Festival girls offer their suitors a knotted scarf. If it holds two red sticks, it means the girl wants a husband. If it contains one red stick, she wants a friend. If it contains a red chilli pepper, then she wants nothing to do with him.

However, in some other cultures, red has been regarded as one of the colours of evil. For instance, medieval European devils are frequently depicted as red, while in the Book of Revelation there is mention of the 'scarlet-coloured beast'.

SEXY RED

In modern Western culture, red can be a feminine sexual statement – rouge 'blusher' makeup has long been used to show fecundity, as have, more recently, red lipstick, red nail varnish and red dresses. Some evolutionary psychologists and socio-biologists have studied the ubiquity of red makeup use among women, and have concluded that its use is 'hard-wired': i.e. an evolved behaviour. The British zoologist and author Desmond Morris has suggested that red lipstick use is an evolutionary adaptation that arose from male apes being turned on by the blood-engorged buttocks of female apes in oestrus. The American evolutionary psychologist Donald Symons hasn't quite gone that far, but has speculated that full red female lips were signals of reproductive fullness and therefore important in sexual signalling, giving red lipstick a kind of evolutionary badge of honour. They call this a 'supernormal' stimulus.

The evidence, however, favours a cultural rather than evolutionary origin, not least because widespread lipstick-wearing only began during the twentieth century, following vigorous advertising campaigns, after tens of thousands of years when most women neglected this strategy. In contemporary Western culture, the feminine sexual connotations of red appear to have a strong pull. For example, in a 2012 study published in the *Journal of Hospitality & Tourism Research*, it was found that service tips given by male customers to waitresses who wore red were 26 per cent higher than those who didn't wear red. Female customers, however, tipped the same, whether the waitress wore red or not.

When we look at the cultural terminology (and clichés) spawned by the colour red, we find that blood, sex and lust are seldom far away. For example, the kind of man who describes himself as a *red-blooded male* might seek out *red-hot sex* in the *red light district*, after *painting the town red* – a nineteenth-century term relating to debauchery, which emerged from the use of bonfires and firecrackers on US Independence Day. And yet he might get *red-hot* with anger if he finds his wife casting her eyes elsewhere. In English it might be said that someone has turned into a green-eyed monster due to jealousy or envy, but the Chinese would talk instead of the *red-eyed monster* – alluding to the fire-breathing dragons of their mythology.

The connotations of red are not always so positive for women. In Nathaniel Hawthorne's 1850 romance *The Scarlet Letter*, set in Puritan seventeenth-century Boston, the beautiful Hester Prynne is accused of adultery and forced to wear a big scarlet letter 'A' (for adulteress) on her way to the gallows. This wasn't fictitious invention. Women convicted of adultery at that time were publicly whipped and had the letter stitched to their clothes. If they removed the letter they were whipped again. Today the term 'scarlet letter'

Sexy in red: The fashion world caught on to the connection between red and sexual allure, demonstrated by the red lipstick and dress of Anita Ekberg (left) and a model from the same era (right).

survives, referring to a symbol of something someone has done wrong in the past, perhaps after being *caught red-handed*, which goes back to fifteenth-century Scotland, referring to those caught with blood on their hands from poaching. (This could leave you *red-faced* with embarrassment.)

The allure of red has changed over time. In *Little Red Riding Hood*, popularized by the Brothers Grimm in 1812, who drew from French and German folklore going back to the 1600s, the red-cloaked girl is conned by the wolf, in granny's clothing, that invites her into bed and then devours her. When Hans Christian Andersen

Left: Hester Prynne was branded as an adulteress in Nathaniel Hawthorne's *The Scarlet Letter*, a punishment that was rooted in reality.

Above: Little Red Riding Hood in her red cloak (left); Karen in her red shoes (right).

wrote *The Red Shoes* in 1845, his message about their power was brutally cautionary. Karen, the high-spirited peasant girl, defies the sage warnings of the rich old woman, succumbs to vanity and buys the red shoes. As soon as she puts them on, they won't stop dancing. Eventually she persuades a woodsman to chop off her feet with the shoes stuck on, and then she dies. Ninety-four years later, in the film version of *The Wizard of Oz*, Dorothy leaves black-and-white Kansas, puts on the sparkling and magical red slippers and goes skipping down the yellow brick road to fulfilment and delight.

WHY DO BULLS SEE RED?

Actually, they don't. Bulls, like dogs and cats, are colour-blind to red – but, back in the day, the bullfighters had no way of knowing this. Tests have since shown that the bull will charge just as ferociously at the blue side of a *toreador*'s muleta cape. It's the waving movement, not the colour, that antagonizes the bull. Red is also convenient for the capes and uniforms of the matador because it doesn't show up the blood – both that of the bull and the matador's.

REVOLUTIONARY RED

One of red's most persistent associations is with the political left – socialism and communism and the blood of revolution. This goes back to the Middle Ages, when fighting ships used red streamer flags to suggest a fight to the death. The first link to protest came in 1293 when a group of English pirates raised a red streamer after disputing the Crown's right to share the bounty of a boat they'd captured. Throughout Europe, red was utilized to show defiance – for example, on castles and cities under siege – but it really came of age during the French Revolution when, in 1789, it was hoisted during the storming of the Bastille, and in 1791, when Lafayette raised a red flag over the Champ de Mars after declaring martial law to warn off rioters, fifty of whom were killed. The Jacobins responded by raising their own red flag to commemorate the 'martyrs' blood' and during the reign of terror that ensued, the red flag became their unofficial emblem. After that, its appeal spread rapidly. When British sailors mutinied in 1797, they hoisted red flags on their ships.

It was first used as a symbol of worker power during the Merthyr Rising in 1831, when marchers in South Wales soaked flags in calf blood. The reputation of defiant red soon crossed the Atlantic Ocean, and was used by the Mexicans during their siege of the Alamo in 1836. A variation on the theme came from Garibaldi during his campaign to unify Italy, when his followers wore red shirts. The banners of the 1848 French revolution, and of the Paris Commune of 1871, were red, after which it became the colour of communism, later to be adopted as the flag of the Soviet Union (with the yellow hammer, sickle and star in the top left corner) and of China (where the rival nationalist party of Chiang Kai-shek also used red to shore up its revolutionary credentials in their losing fight against Mao's Red Army).

By the time the British Labour Party was founded in 1906, the reputation of red as the colour of the left was well on its way to being entrenched, so they adopted the red flag as their emblem, but eighty years later, a switch was made to the red rose. However, delegates at Labour Party conferences continue to sing 'The Red Flag', a song written in 1889. In 1976, Labour Party MPs burst into a hearty rendition, prompting the Tory

Opposite, clockwise: French revolutionaries storming the Bastille; Garibaldi with his men; a mass demonstration on National Day outside the Gate of Heavenly Peace, Tiananmen, China, during the Cultural Revolution of the late 1960s; a parade celebrating the fifty-ninth anniversary of the Russian Bolshevik Revolution, Moscow, 1976.

GARIBALDI.
Entrée à Naples.

Left: Communist red combined with the hammer, sickle and star of the Soviet Union, which Lenin stands in front of proudly.

notable, Michael Heseltine, to swing the parliamentary mace above his head in exasperation. With the decline of communism it lost its power to shock, but its lyrics still give a neat illustration of the links between flag, colour and blood:

> The people's flag is deepest red,
> It shrouded oft our martyred dead,
> And ere their limbs grew stiff and cold,
> Their hearts' blood dyed its every fold.
> So raise the scarlet standard high,
> Beneath its shade we'll live and die,
> Though cowards flinch and traitors sneer,
> We'll keep the red flag flying here.

Beyond the UK, red retains a vestige of its former power. In 2016, after Brazil's left-of-centre president Dilma Rousseff was unseated, in what some called a constitutional coup, there were several news reports of children riding red bicycles or wearing red shirts, being chased and assaulted by anti-left thugs.

Red has a special place in the politics of the United States. 'The Red Flag' song found its way there a decade after it was composed, and in 1909 was featured in the *Little Red Songbook* of the 'Wobblies' (the Industrial Workers of the World), a collection of their tunes, songs and hymns. But far more potent was the American backlash against all things red, which picked up momentum after the First World War, with several states banning the display of red flags, only to have these actions declared unconstitutional by the Supreme Court. In the 1950s, McCarthyite America lived in fear of the 'Red Peril' and 'Reds under the Bed' – terms drawn from the fear of 'red' communism.

There's an odd anomaly in the colours of US political parties: the usually right-of-centre Republican Party has red as its colour, while the occasionally left-of-centre Democrat Party has blue. In Britain, Germany, Austria, Ireland, Romania, Taiwan and Canada, however, blue is the colour of conservatism.

This is a recent thing – in fact, until the late 1990s it tended to go in the opposite direction. But in the 2000 presidential election that brought George W. Bush to power, the NBC television pundit Tim Russert used red for Republican states and blue for Democratic states and it just stuck. Blue had been used for Democrats in Texas in the late nineteenth century, and early in the twentieth century *The New York Times* and the *Washington Post* used blue for Democratic states. But it was only after 2000 that media outlets began to conform, leading pundits to talk of 'red states' (Republican), 'blue states' (Democrat) and sometimes 'purple states' (hard to call). When *The New York Times* graphics editor explained their choice he said it was because both *Republican* and *red* begin with the letter R.

WHY RED-LETTER DAYS?

It originated in 509 BC when Roman calendars marked important days in red. This practice was revived in medieval Europe with capital letters and important words highlighted in red, and continued after the invention of the printing press. Later, holidays were marked in calendars in red, and the term red-letter day became associated with any day that was significant.

ARISTOCRATIC RED

Not all historical references to the colour red are drawn from the elements of blood, fire and sex. The origin of aristocratic red has a very different story, relating to money, status and power.

For much of human history people did not wear coloured clothes. The transition from hunter-gatherer lifestyles to agriculture, which started around 10,000 years ago, prompted a transition from skins and furs to fabrics, although this shift was gradual and took thousands of years. The business of dyeing these clothes was exceedingly tricky and took thousands more years to take root. With some colours the dyes washed out with the first drop of rain, and those that didn't were expensive to produce. Red dye was a case in point. The best red dye was produced by extracting carmine dye from the cochineal scale insect, which is native to the Americas and feeds on the leaves of the prickly pear cactus.

The founders of this dyeing technique were the Aztecs, Incas and Maya, who also used cochineal for medicine, adornment and painting. Cochineal also had religious significance. For example, the Inca believed that their goddess Mama Huaco emerged from the Paqariq Tampu cave in Peru wearing red. The Spanish conquistadors, under the command of Hernán Cortés (1485–1547), were dazzled by the brilliant red of Aztec clothing and, after acquiring the recipes from their colonial subjects, they set them to work on producing huge quantities of this wonderful, colourfast red dye, earning a fortune for king and country.

For two centuries the Spanish kept the process secret, partly by spreading charming rumours about the existence of a versatile little animal that was part-fruit, part-worm, which they called a wormberry. Their export of cochineal dye from Mexico rose from 50 tons a year at the beginning of the sixteenth century to 160 tons at the end. But eventually, in 1777, the secret got out when one Thierry de Mononville, a twenty-five-year-old Frenchman, smuggled out a cactus covered with cochineal insects, took it to Port au Prince, in Haiti, and set to work farming them.

Still, the dye remained prohibitively expensive because it took 150,000 of the tiny insects to produce a single kilogram of dye. They had to be dried and crushed to obtain the pigment, which was then mixed with alum. So it was hardly surprising that

Opposite: The last Aztec ruler, Moctezuma II, standing proudly in his cochineal red cloak, before being imprisoned by Spanish conquistador Hernán Cortés.

only the aristocracy and the super-rich could afford red clothes, carpets and wall hangings. But it wasn't just about cost. All over the world, from at least the time of the Ancient Greeks, Romans and Chinese, powers and principalities introduced sumptuary laws that placed restrictions on the clothes, colours and jewellery people could wear, depending on status, class and gender. It was one of the ways they enforced their hierarchies.

Post-Roman European sumptuary laws were applied in Italy and France from the 1500s, but they were most vigorous in England, starting with Richard I – also known as Richard the Lionheart. He introduced a ruling, in 1197, that restricted the masses to wearing only grey clothing which, for most, was not much of a restriction because the only clothes they possessed were made from rough, undyed grey cloth.

In later centuries, as dyes became more available, commoners were restricted to a narrow range of their own earthy colours. Although these laws were not always rigorously enforced, there were periodic calls for implementation – particularly during the Elizabethan era. In some cases, failure to comply could lead to fines, loss of property and title, imprisonment and even death – although there are no reports of executions for wearing the wrong colour clothes.

There were also laws in some European countries against mixing colours, which, in the Middle Ages, was seen as part of the dark art of alchemy. So, for example, mixing blue and yellow dye to create green was strictly forbidden, and those working in black and blue were restricted, by their guilds, from working in red and yellow.

The main purpose of the sumptuary laws was to indicate status in those wearing one colour or another, and to keep the newly wealthy merchants separate from the land-owning nobility. These laws were publicly motivated by a call to prevent excess, waste, vanity and moral decay among common people. They had the secondary purpose of encouraging commoners to spend their money in certain ways. For example, in order to stimulate English wool production, a new sumptuary law was introduced in 1571 compelling all non-noble males over the age of six to wear woollen caps on Sundays and holidays. Failure to comply invited a stiff fine.

Under these laws, red colours were solely for the highest nobility, along with gold, silver, dark blue, black and pure white. Only royalty were allowed to wear purple. Commoners were restricted to earthy colours, such as greys, browns, yellows, greens and oranges, and also pale blue and pale red (which centuries later would be called pink).

By the end of the seventeenth century sumptuary laws all over Europe had been repealed or had fallen into disuse. Red, however, remained the preserve of the noblemen, cardinals and wealthy merchants simply because of the cost of the cochineal dyeing process.

It took until the 1870s before a cheap, colourfast substitute was found: a new synthetic dye called alizarin. In no time, red lost its aristocratic status and came to be seen as flash, vulgar and erotic. But one aspect of its past splendour survives: the

Left: Red was a colour solely reserved for the aristocracy for hundreds of years.

red carpet. The first reference to its use comes in the Greek play *Agamemnon* by Aeschylus. The eponymous Agamemnon returns from Troy and his wife invites him to step on to the crimson carpet she has laid. It has become a tradition in the modern world, ever since a red carpet was rolled out to welcome US President James Monroe in Georgetown, South Carolina, 1821, to prevent his feet from getting muddy on a riverbank. Today it is used for everyone from Popes to Oscar winners and the term 'rolling out the red carpet' has become a metaphor for an effusive welcome.

STARBUCKS AND THE COCHINEAL REVIVAL

By the twentieth century, colourfast synthetic red dyes were a dime-a-dozen, but safe red food and cosmetic dyes remained a problem. Many of the dyes used turned out to be carcinogenic, so the search for a safe red food colouring led back to the cochineal insect. Under the code number E120, it began to appear in lipsticks, rouge, face powders, blusher and eye-shadows, as well as in jams, maraschino cherries, sausage skins, some alcoholic drinks and also in the 'Strawberries and Crème Frappuccino' made by Starbucks.

This might be fine for anyone worried about carcinogenic 'e-numbers', but not so much for people more worried about purity in their vegetarianism or veganism, or for those a bit squeamish about ingesting insects. In 2012 some bloggers were outraged to discover that E120 was really cochineal pigment and set up an online petition against Starbucks. It took a mere 6,500 signatures before the Seattle-based company capitulated and announced that cochineal would be replaced by a tomato extract. Cochineal is still widely used in lipstick and other cosmetics and in some food products. It has since been found that although the cochineal pigment is indeed non-carcinogenic, it can cause allergic reactions.

SANTA CLAUS AND RED

A red Santa is often said to be the work of the Coca-Cola Company, but this is not quite true – or not the full truth. The original Saint Nicholas, the kindly fourth-century bishop who gave rise to Santa Claus, is said to have dressed in ecclesiastical red, though there is some debate about this. So when Saint Nicholas made his first appearance in the Middle Ages, he was frequently depicted dressed in red, but quite often in green too. Over the years, across Europe there were also Santas shown clad in brown and several other colours, but by the nineteenth century red had become commonplace. The current image of Santa is the work of the Swedish illustrator Haddon Sundblom, who was hired by Coca-Cola for a series of advertisements. He chose a fat, jolly Santa, with a red coat trimmed with white ermine, which just happened to fit with the branding colours of Coke. Red and white were taken from the red and white flag of Peru, the source of its coca leaves, which were part of the recipe until the 1920s.

ORANGE

A CHRISTINA ROSSETTI POEM tells of the rich natural associations of all the colours bar one: orange. 'What is Pink' ends with: 'What is orange? Why an orange / Just an orange!' In fact, the colour orange is about much more than orange the fruit. Nature often displays the colour orange, from sunsets and flowers and spices to a wonderful range of fruits and vegetables, and yet Rossetti was right in one respect: it is the only colour in the English language where the name comes from a fruit. There are other languages where the name of colour and fruit are separated: for example, in Afrikaans, the word for the fruit is *lemoen*, but the name for the colour is *oranje*.

In the paint mixing tray orange is, of course, formed by blending red with yellow, but as a unique pigment, it is a relatively recent addition to the paintbox: cadmium red and chrome orange were only discovered about 200 years ago. The word 'orange' is also a relatively recent addition to English. There are still several languages that have no word for the colour, including Himba, Nafana and Piraha. This is perhaps part of the reason why its connotations are more confined than its companions – to the sunny optimism of its warmth, a disparate range of political identities and as a colour of high visibility, used for traffic cones, life vests, dangerous machinery and the 'black boxes' of aeroplanes.

THE JOURNEY OF ORANGE

Oranges were first cultivated in China around 4,500 years ago and they slowly travelled west, via the Silk Road. The word 'orange' has its origins in an ancient Dravidian language, from southern India, from a word meaning 'fragrant'.

Above: Oranges have been cultivated for thousands of years, and their slow journey west meant many languages along their path have similar-sounding words for the fruit.

From there it went to Sanskrit, where the term for an orange tree – *narangah* – served as the root for many languages' translations of the word as it travelled wherever oranges were planted and sold, hence its similar sound in various languages: *naranga* in India, *narang* in Farsi, *naranj* in Arabic and *naranja* in Spanish.

In English the word 'orange' is a corruption of the Sanskrit. People mistook 'a *naranga*' to be 'an *aranga*', so it evolved into 'an orange'. The same thing happened to the name of the viper snake 'adder', which evolved from the Middle English 'a *naddre*', thus becoming 'an *adder*'.

The only English word for 'orange' before the fruit arrived was *geoluread*, meaning 'yellow-red'. It wasn't until the sixteenth century that the word orange came into common usage and became the name of the colour, because the fruit was definitively orange in colour.

THE ODD POLITICS OF ORANGE

When orange enters the sphere of politics and nations it bristles with meanings unrelated to fruit or colour, but still somehow overlaps with them. In the Netherlands today it is the colour of benign celebration. Every 27 April, millions of Hollanders dress up in orange to celebrate their king's day and have a wonderful time. Yet when it comes to geopolitics, tribal identity and national pride, orange has long been a major player.

It all goes back to 105 BC, when the Romans fought the Celts in Aurasio (named after a Celtic water god) in Provence, France, leading to the establishment of the colony of Aurasio. The name became linguistically conflated with the then word for orange, leading to the Ancient Diocese of Orange at the end of the third century AD. Subsequently, it became the Principality of Orange as a fiefdom of the Holy Roman Empire in the twelfth century. The originally Dutch-German Orange-Nassau dynasty then acquired land in Provence, including the Principality of Orange. This leads us up to 1544, when the title 'Prince of Orange' passed to William I of Orange, who led the Dutch revolt against Spanish rule, eventually winning Dutch independence, under the House of Orange-Nassau. After the 1688 anti-Catholic invasion of England

Opposite (top): Dutch people celebrate *Koningsdag*, their king's birthday, a national holiday, in traditional orange. (Bottom) A map of the principality of Orange.

46

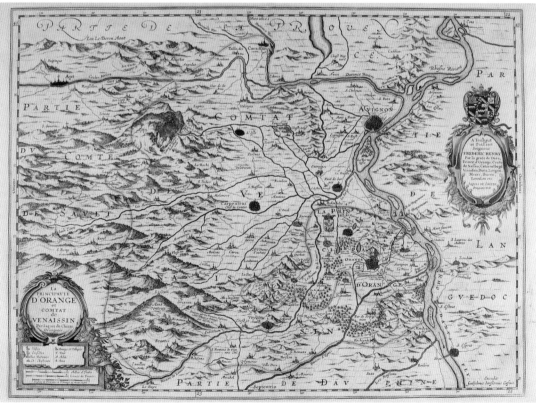

known as the 'Glorious Revolution', William III of Orange became king of England, Scotland and Ireland.

A year later 'King Billy' (William III – incidentally the third of his name for both Orange and England; in Scotland he was known as William II) vanquished the deposed James II at the Battle of the Boyne in Ireland, in which at least 2,000 soldiers died and 50,000 were wounded, securing the dominance of Irish Protestants and the suppression of Irish Catholics for the next three centuries. In honour of William III, the victorious Protestant king they exalted, orange became the colour of Ireland's Royalists, who formed an organization – The Orange Order – to assert their identity as loyalist Protestant subjects of the monarchy. Their opponents were the Republicans, who later adopted green as their colour. In 1922, the Irish Free State was eventually secured, so winning the Catholic-based Republicans part of their dream, as a compromise. Their new tri-colour flag contained Gaelic green on the one side, Royalist orange on the other, with white in the middle to symbolize peace.

Meanwhile, Holland's colonial conquests fell under the Orange Standard. One of these, forged by the Dutch East India Company, was the Cape of Good Hope, but after the British took this outpost during the Napoleonic wars, Dutch-speaking settlers trekked north and used their muskets to relieve the Africans of their historical land. Among the territories they seized in the mid-nineteenth century was one they called the *Oranje-Vrystaat* (Orange Free State). The farmers who settled there, with their orange and white flag, were among those who later fought the Anglo-Boer War against the soldiers of a state headed by an English king, with family ties to the descendants of the old House of Orange.

To complicate matters further, these Protestant Dutch descendants were supported by Catholic Irish Republicans, who, in turn, were fighting their own battles against the Protestant Orangemen at home in Ireland. Decades later, when the South African apartheid state, whose flag included a band of Dutch orange, was fighting a losing battle for survival, it sent hit-men to make common cause with Ulster's Orange terrorists, who were fighting against the 'green-tinged' descendants of the Republicans, their old allies, who had backed the 'orange-tinged' Boers ninety years before.

All very perplexing, and just to confuse matters further, by the time the green Irish had embraced orange for their country's flag, the orange Dutch had long since abandoned it. This had nothing to do, however, with politics and everything to do with weather, dye and common sense. The old Dutch flag had orange, white and blue stripes. The problem was that because of the instability of the

vegetable dyes – mixing red and yellow – the orange stripe had a habit of turning red in the sun and rain. The Dutch were a practical people, so from about 1630 they settled for red instead of orange.

Today the Dutch flag is therefore red, white and blue although the old orange, white and blue flags continued to be used at sea for a while longer, which is why these colours were found in the flags of some of Holland's former colonies. One of the colonies was New York City, which was founded by the Dutch as New Amsterdam but was later lost to the English, who first called it New York, and was briefly called New Orange when, in 1673, the English lost the city and the third Anglo-Dutch War. However, a year later the two countries signed the Treaty of Westminster. The city returned to English rule, and it became New York again, although the flag retained its vertical orange stripe, as did the flag of Albany, New York. Orange continues to be a peculiarly Dutch colour, used in all their national celebrations and by their sports teams, although today's version is lighter and brighter than that of old.

Below: The Boers, Dutch descendants of the Orange Free State, fighting the British.

ORANGEMEN AND BOWLER HATS

The Orange Order was founded in 1795 as a kind of Masonic brotherhood devoted to Protestantism and British rule. The name was a tribute to the Dutchman William III, who assured the ascendancy of Ireland's Protestants by winning the Battle of the Boyne. In the nineteenth century they took to wearing orange sashes on their annual marches, as had William's troops, while the bowler hat was adopted in the early twentieth as a symbol of British authority because it was worn as work dress by Queen's Guard officers, City gents and Northern Irish dock foremen. Orangemen – 'Orangewomen' are not allowed – also wear dark suits and white gloves, and carry orange banners celebrating King William III.

Left: Orangemen on their annual march, sporting their traditional regalia.

ORANGE ON THE FIELD

Sometimes people take the connotations of colours too literally – and orange is no exception. A team of anthropologists, from Durham and Plymouth Universities, decided to embark on a bit of odd research – examining the home colours of football clubs to see which did best, in terms of team performance. Red came out top, orange, bottom. Professor Robert Barton from Durham University explained his hypothesis to the BBC: 'Firstly, over time supporters may have been subconsciously attracted to a club wearing red, so the club has developed an increasing resource base within its community. Secondly, there may be a positive psychological boost from wearing red that is reflected on the field of play. Competing against a team in red could also impair performance.'

Alternatively, it could have nothing to do with the above, because correlation and causation are not the same thing. The colours chosen by clubs go deep into their histories, and their supporters choose them for a wide range of reasons. Teams rise and fall through the rankings regardless of colour.

The most successful team wearing orange is probably the two-time NFL-winning American gridiron football club, the Miami Dolphins. In international 'soccer', we have Ivory Coast, whose third African Cup of Nations triumph came in 2015 and, of course, the Netherlands, who proudly play in orange, as do their very successful darts players.

WHAT HAPPENED TO THE ORANGE KINGS?

Orange kings and queens have happily survived in the Netherlands, but in England, Scotland and Ireland there was just one: William III, who usurped King James II to become English king after the Glorious Revolution. He and his English wife, Mary, were crowned together, as joint sovereigns, in 1689. Mary died of smallpox in 1694, so William ruled alone. He was said to be gay, and was childless, which meant that when he died, of pneumonia in 1702 following a fall from his horse, he had no successors. Thus the English crown went from Dutch-speaking William III, via his English sister-in-law, Anne, who ruled for twelve years, to Hanoverian George I, who spoke only German.

CANELO AND GINGER SPICE

Mexico's most popular sportsman is a professional boxer called *Canelo*, which means 'cinnamon'. His real name is Saul Álvarez and he's an outstanding fighting machine. One of the main reasons for his extraordinary appeal is his orange hair, which is unusual in his part of the world. *Canelo* is widely considered an object of beauty, a sex symbol, a man to be looked at and admired; and his red crown is part of it.

In Britain, for example, about 4 per cent – one in twenty-five – of the population have phenotypic red hair. This compares with about 1 per cent in other Western populations. Some 28 per cent of the British population carry the 'red' hair allele without expression: i.e. they are genotypic. There are various pejorative names for people with orange or red hair, as some people are inclined to single-out and hector them for looking different.

There is a rich history of heroic 'redheads', including Boudicca, Henry VIII, Christopher Columbus, Thomas Jefferson, Florence Nightingale and Marilyn Monroe before she dyed it blonde. Yet literature is full of examples of prejudicial attitudes towards such people. They are often portrayed as devious, criminally inclined, sexually promiscuous and quick-tempered, hence the terms 'hot-headed' and 'fiery', in allusion to the hair having flame-like colouring.

WHAT IS A CLOCKWORK ORANGE?

Anthony Burgess's violent, dystopian 1962 novel took its title from a Cockney phrase referring to something that is strange internally but appears normal on the surface. Burgess took it to refer to someone who can only perform good or evil, and noted in the introduction to the 1988 edition that this meant 'he has the appearance of an organism lovely with colour and juice, but is in fact only a clockwork toy to be wound up by God or the Devil or (since this is increasingly replacing both) the Almighty State'. In other words, it was a comment on the decay of society, as Burgess saw it.

This was satirized by Jonathan Swift in *Gulliver's Travels*: 'It is observed that the red-haired of both sexes are more libidinous and mischievous than the rest,' he writes with tongue in cheek. The idea that there is some natural link between red hair and ill-temper is the most common trope, but moral weakness comes a close second.

While these attitudes have deep historical roots, they appear to have become worse in the new millennium, almost as if it's the last form of xenophobia tolerated. Over the past two decades there have been several reported crimes of violence against redheads, and at least one case of a schoolboy committing suicide after sustained bullying because of his hair colour.

Right: Saul 'Canelo' Álvarez, a world-champion boxer, is one of the few Mexicans with naturally orange hair.

Of course, redheads don't often have 'orange' hair as such, as it varies a great deal in colour and tone. It ranges from 'strawberry blonde', through dazzling marmalade orange, to auburn, copper and dark burgundy. It may have started among humans through limited breeding with Neanderthals, as DNA samples have shown that some Neanderthals had bright orange hair. Its spread may have been influenced by natural selection because it occurs more often among people living in colder regions of northern Europe, and is accompanied by the lightest of skin and eye colours, as well as freckles and a high sensitivity to ultraviolet light. That is to say, it began as a mutation but was not selected out of the gene pool because the environment meant that those with the redhead gene were not at a disadvantage as they would have been in warmer climates.

Ireland has the highest incidence of redheads, accounting for around 10 per cent of the population. Scotland is second with 7 per cent. There is also a 'hot spot' of redheads in the Volga region of Russia, due to a population known as the Udmurt people.

Such strongholds for certain genetic traits can be due to genetic drift. This occurs when a trait produced by random genetic mutation takes root in small, isolated groups of people without conferring any evolutionary advantage or disadvantage, and then spreads due to its neutrality. The fact that most redhead populations come in geographic clusters suggests that genetic drift has been involved. There are pockets of redheads in parts of China and other areas of Asia. In Polynesia, where it doesn't cause pale skin, it is traditionally seen as a sign of leadership and noble descent. There are various genetic types, but red hair is most commonly caused by two copies of a recessive allele on chromosome 16. This produces a particular protein responsible for the pigment pheomelanin, which causes red hair.

BUDDHISTS, HARI KRISHNAS AND ORANGE

The robes worn by Buddhist monks (right) are said to symbolize modesty and simplicity, but the colour orange itself has no particular significance. The earliest monks in Thailand chose orange because orange dye from the heartwood of the jackfruit tree was freely available. The colour was later adopted by Hari Krishna devotees. Their 'saffron robes' are not really dyed with saffron, which is exorbitantly expensive – currently around £7,200 a kilogram. The high price tag for this spice is due to the labour-intensive process of extracting stigmas from saffron crocus flowers.

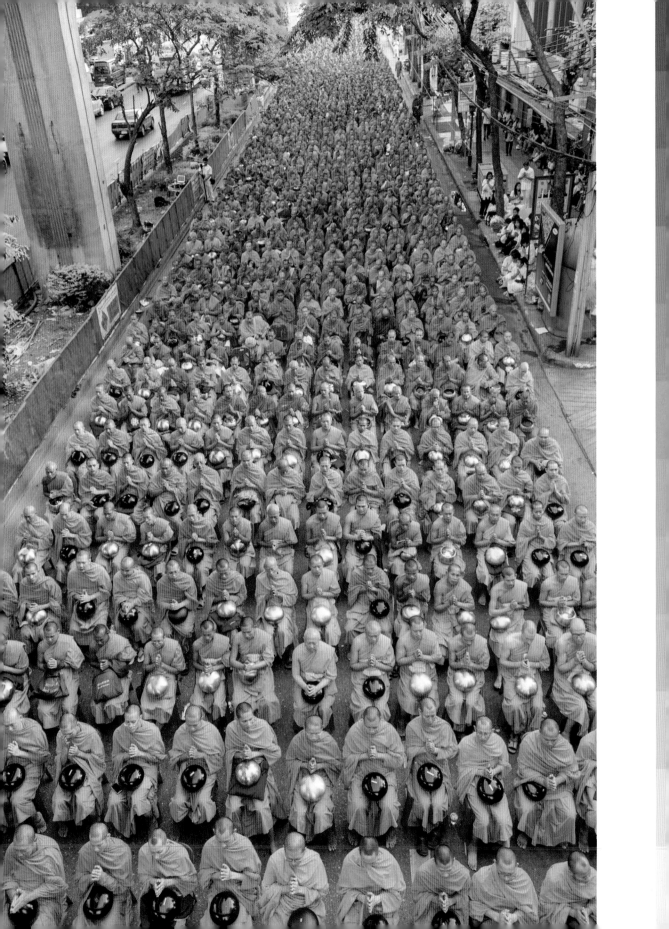

BROWN

BROWN IS A STRANGELY anonymous colour. Like pink, one won't find it in the rainbow or the colour wheel but unlike pink, one also won't find it in most books on colour. When looked at in terms of light it occupies the space between yellow and orange, albeit with less brightness, and in the paintbox it is made by mixing the primary colours (or adding blue to orange). So brown deserves its place – a proper colour, unlike black, white, grey and gold – and yet when one asks someone to list the main colours, the chances are that brown will be forgotten.

This is odd because its credentials, both positive and negative, are impressive. Alongside green, it is one of the main colours of nature and it suggests a warm and homely feel – the colour of our floors and furniture and much of what we eat. In terms of fashion, brown is often found in leather, from handbags to belts, yet has picked up unfavourable reviews in certain job sectors, especially when used in suits, shirts and shoes.

THE BROWN MAJORITY

The range of shades that qualify as brown is wider than with any other colour. The reason is that brown can describe a wide range of tertiary colours: those that contain all three primary colours of red, blue and yellow. Therefore, there is no definitive brown colour. Any colour, from fawn to ebony can fall under 'brown'. Thus we have mud brown, chestnut brown, tan brown, chocolate brown, beige brown, mousy brown, rich brown, coffee brown, rusty brown, straw brown, burnt brown and many other descriptions for the colour.

Brown's range of shades has long been used as a racial stereotype for skin colour for a number of ethnicities. In evolutionary terms, the emergence of 'white' skin is a recent event. The lighter one's skin, the more vitamin D it synthesizes from sunlight. Natural selection therefore meant people became lighter in more northerly regions (they were more likely to survive and reproduce because they were less likely to get the vitamin D deficiency disease, rickets). But until around 5,000 years ago, after agriculture had replaced hunting and gathering as the main source of food for humans, Europeans were much darker skinned, although some had already evolved to have blue eyes by then (DNA taken from the 5,000-year-old remains of a European hunter-gatherer showed that while he had dark skin, his eyes were blue). But the advent of agriculture meant a changed diet, which in turn increased evolutionary pressure for lighter skin (because fewer foods rich in vitamin D increased the need to obtain vitamin D using sunlight, which meant that people with lighter skin had the selective edge). It is also likely that natural selection ensured skins became darker in parts of Africa when people moved closer to the equator because those born with cancer-protecting, melanin-rich dark skin were more likely to have longer lives.

Right: Before the start of agriculture in Europe, the inhabitants of the region were found to have dark skin, dark hair and blue eyes, a look that no longer exists.

Following page: One of the Benin bronzes, said to have been made by the 'Hamites'.

When we look at the human genome, differences in skin colour, eye colour and hair colour represent minute genetic distinctions, and yet this tiny detail was magnified through slavery and colonial conquest, encouraging the belief that 'brown' skin conveyed profound messages about innate intelligence and character. Those with darker skins, particularly of African origin, were called 'black', and well into the twentieth century people with power and influence were all too eager to discuss what they felt this skin colour implied. For example, Karl Jung, the German-Swiss psychologist, considered adult Africans' intelligence to be much lower than that of Europeans, and visited Kenya in 1925 to carry out a 'scientific inquiry' to try to prove this. In Jung's time, there was still a widely held view that all the most obvious achievements of pre-colonial Africa – from the Benin bronzes to Great Zimbabwe – must have been the result of a paler people they called the 'Hamites' (named after the Biblical Ham, son of Noah) because people with dark skins couldn't possibly have produced such works. The Hamites did not, in fact, exist.

Over the years, 'science' added to the misconceptions around the significance of brown skin. In the nineteenth century there was an obsession with head size and brain weight, with scientists sometimes comparing those of light-skinned men and dark-skinned women before concluding there was a link between darker skins, smaller heads and lower intelligence. They then took to finding ways of measuring what was inside those heads, and divided the results into categories relating to skin colour and regional origin. Their tool was the IQ test, which they thought measured inbuilt intelligence. When they found differences in average IQ between population groups, they decided this proved their point.

It later emerged that while IQ could measure a kind of abstract logic, it was highly susceptible to environmental influence. While all IQs were rising generation on generation because people were being exposed to more and more abstraction, the IQs of some groups were rising faster than others because of changed cultural circumstances. In the 1950s, Asian Americans had lower IQs than average but by the 1980s their IQs were above average. American Jewish IQs were below average during the First World War but above by the Second World War. And the IQs of African Americans were rising faster than those of white Americans. The most rapid recorded rise was among rural Kenyan children – an increase of 26.3 IQ points in fourteen years. Studies of identical twins who, for various reasons, were separated but raised in different class and educational backgrounds, found their IQs could vary by as much as 30 points.

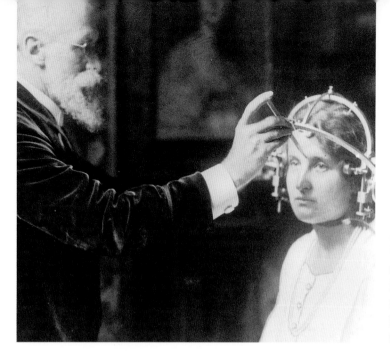

Left: A professor at Humboldt University in Berlin uses a specially designed instrument to measure head mass and the shape of the skull, which was thought to give indicators of innate levels of intelligence.

So, the misconception that skin colour has any bearing on intelligence (or any other character trait) has been put to bed by science, and yet prejudices along these lines linger and still occasionally find their way into pop psychology and pop science tomes.

BROWN CLOTHES

There is some modern prejudice against wearing brown, especially in the workplace. In 2016, a study by the British government's Social Mobility Commission found that first-class graduates from top universities, who came from working-class backgrounds, were being locked out of top jobs for sartorial sins like wearing brown shoes. The commission's head, Alan Milburn, said: 'Some investment bank managers still judge candidates on whether they wear brown shoes with a suit, rather than on their skills and potential.' The adage, 'Never wear brown in town' is even more rigid when it comes to suits for bankers and lawyers working in major capital cities.

This comes from a young attorney about to start work at an eminent City law firm. 'The wife of a top lawyer gave me some sartorial advice. "My dear, never wear a white shirt, and never, never be seen in a brown suit – that would be unforgivable."' Beyond the financial sector, the admonitions against brown clothes are slowly being reversed, as trends for brown suits and shoes have emerged in recent times.

Historically, brown has fared little better. Wearing a brown shirt, for instance, particularly one that looks a bit military in terms of its style, might raise some eyebrows. The Nazi *Sturmabteilung* became known as the 'Brownshirts' because of the colour of their

Right: Propaganda poster announcing a political campaign for the Nazi party in Germany, showing two brown-shirted soldiers.

uniforms (chosen because in Germany brown army shirts were cheap after the First World War). The role of these brown-shirted 'Stormtroopers' in the 1920s and early 1930s included disrupting meetings of opponents and general intimidation of those whom the Nazis did not view as suitably 'German'. When the Nazis won power in 1933 it was known as the 'Brown Revolution', and pro-Nazi areas were said to have 'voted brown'. The Stormtroopers made way for the even more notorious SS in 1934 but, by then, brown had become a preferred Nazi colour. Indeed, their Munich headquarters was called the 'Brown House'.

One form of brown is a fashion perennial, however, and has few of the negative connotations of the brown suit or shirt: khaki. This variant of light brown (with a hint of yellow) has long been the colour of military uniforms all over the world – starting in 1848 when the word 'khaki' was borrowed from Hindi (it means 'soil-coloured').

Khaki uniforms proved more practical and significantly less visible than the old red coats of the British military, for example (which were great for hiding blood, but not so much if you wanted to hide from bullets). After the Second World War 'khakis' also became popular for civilian leisurewear trousers and shorts, and they remain so today, for both men and women, in various fabrics and shades.

Right: From the original use of the Hindi word khaki and the colour's employment in old military uniforms (which still endures in India, see picture at start of chapter), the colour has taken on a new lease of life in modern fashion.

WHAT DOES 'BROWNED-OFF' MEAN?

Browned-off means annoyed. It started as an agricultural term meaning 'ruined'. An 1883 *Oxford Journal* report on a Canterbury fruit harvest noted: 'Fortunately the weather has been damp … because otherwise the remaining fruit would have been "browned off" and rendered useless.' It became popular more than 100 years ago as an army term for being fed-up, as an alternative to 'brassed-off', which was a term used by servants who were tasked with polishing the brass.

BROWNIES

It's a name shared by cake-like treats, compulsive little elves – who insist on tidying up when one is asleep – and junior girl guides or girl scouts. Brownie elves started out in Scottish and northern English folklore as wrinkly little fellows, with curly brown hair and brown cloaks and hoods who inhabited houses, hiding in attics and holes, and cleaning up at night in exchange for little 'gifts' of food (they're particularly fond of porridge and honey). Their equivalents are the Scandinavian *tomte* or *nisse*, the German *Heinzelmännchen* and the Slavic *domovoi*. The most famous modern brownie is Enid Blyton's 1949 creation, Big-Ears (a wise but rather irascible one who served as Noddy's mentor, and lived in a toadstool outside Toytown).

The junior Girl Guides took the name Brownies in 1918 when they complained to their patron, Lady Baden-Powell, that they didn't like being called the Rosebuds. Baden-Powell's revised choice came from an 1870 story, *The Brownies*, about two children who could be helpful like the little elf brownies, or lazy boggarts. The Girl Guide Brownies earned credit for good deeds, prompting the phrase, 'brownie points' from the 1950s.

WHAT IS THE MOST COMMON COLOUR-BASED SURNAME?

Brown, by a long way in English-speaking countries. It is the fourth most common surname in America, Australia and New Zealand and the fifth most common in Canada and Britain. On the colourful surname list, Brown is followed by White, and then Green, Gray/Grey, Black, Scarlet and Blue. The surnames Reid, Read, Reed and Reade all come from the Old English 'Red'. Put them together and they come in fourth place on the colour-based list.

The various interpretations of brownies: a group of brownies (Girl Guides) listening to Brown Owl, their adult leader (right), a Norwegian *nisse* enjoying its Christmas treat in return for its work (below left), and a British brownie undertaking its household chores (below right).

YELLOW

YELLOW IS THE MOST VERSATILE of colours. While red is paired with heat, danger and blood, and blue with the cold and its soothing effects, the third primary colour is whatever you make of it. In much of the West, yellow has become the colour of cowardice, but in the East it suggests heroism and all sorts of happy things. In Japan warriors wore yellow chrysanthemum flowers in battle during the fourteenth century.

In the West, yellow is also the colour of disreputable journalism, and in its 'yellow-dog' form, refers to a contemptible person. In Germany and France people go yellow with envy, and in German a good bruising would leave one 'green and yellow', rather than 'black and blue'.

In France a man who has discovered that his wife has run off with another man might be said to be *jaune cocu* (yellow deceived). In Hindi a woman is said to 'get her hands yellow' when she gets married. To give the bridal couple a healthy, wealthy life they and their gifts are smeared with yellow turmeric before the wedding. Many Indians carry yellow talismans to protect them from illness and misfortune.

THE COLOUR OF COWARDICE

Yellow went into decline for several centuries in medieval times because it was seen as an unwanted and negative sub-white, or dirty white. European paintings from the time conveyed their low regard for the colour by portraying Judas Iscariot wearing yellow to reinforce his image of doomed duplicity. In theatre and art yellow was the colour of hypocrisy, dishonesty and sin, used to portray heretics, assassins, forgers and the like. In France, particularly in the tenth century, traitors and criminals had their doors painted yellow as a sign of their ignominy while actors playing dead were frequently dressed in yellow, and in Spain it was the colour worn by executioners. This is because human

Right: *The Kiss of Judas* by Giotto, which paints its title character in unflattering yellow.

70

corpses turn a yellowish hue when the blood is drained from the skin by gravity. In Farsi, the term 'yellow face' indicates weakness and fear, and in early Islamic depictions it is the colour used to portray nasty people.

The origins of this negativity are opaque but the specific associations with cowardice could come from early medicine, when one of the four bodily 'humours' was yellow bile, which was believed to make one peevish. People suffering from jaundice went a bit yellow and felt bilious, not a condition associated with courage. The term 'chicken', in describing cowardice, probably comes from the yellowish skin of the plucked bird and the fact that chickens tend to panic and run at the slightest sign of danger. Some think it comes from their yellow chicks, but only white hens have yellow chicks and these had not been bred in the 1500s when the term came into use.

The term 'yellow belly' begins with eighteenth century English slang – again a reference to bile and queasiness. In 1842 an American newspaper referred to Mexican soldiers as 'yellow bellied', but the insult only came into common American parlance after the First World War.

YELLOW STARS

Yellow has long been used as the colour of the most virulent forms of anti-Semitism and xenophobia. Jews and Christians got along more or less peacefully under Islamic rule, but the Caliph in early eighth century Medina ordered Jews and Christians to wear yellow badges, as did subsequent Muslim leaders in Baghdad. This was extended to Hindus under Islamic rule in India in the sixteenth century, a practice also enforced on Hindus in Afghanistan under Taliban rule at the end of the last century. Why yellow? Because yellow is viewed as a colour worn by non-believers.

In France, Louis IX ordered Jews to wear yellow pointed hats and, later, round yellow patches. (The painting at the start of this chapter, by Carl Gustaf Hellqvist, shows a Jewish merchant to the

Above: A yellow Star of David badge, worn by Jewish prisoners under the Nazis.

right of the image wearing a *Judenhut*, a yellow hat designed to make Jewish people stand out.) This practice crossed the Channel and was adopted by the brutal Englishman, King Edward I, who took time off from fighting the Scots and Welsh to issue a law in 1274 requiring Jews over the age of seven to wear a yellow patch, before expelling them from England sixteen years later.

Several Popes adopted this practice too – for example, in 1555, Pope Paul IV decreed that all Jews should wear yellow hats. After the invasion of Poland in 1939, the Nazis required Jews to wear a yellow Star of David with the word 'Jew' sewn on, as a prelude to sending them to the concentration camps.

YELLOW SUBMARINES

Yellow was rehabilitated during the Renaissance, and it began to shed its negative meanings and acquire positive ones. Surveys conducted in the United States, Canada and in European countries suggest that despite the cowardice connotation, people in the West tend to associate yellow with spontaneity, gentleness and fun, although only a small fraction – around 6 per cent – cited it as their favourite colour.

The colour developed happy associations with the music of the counter-culture in the 1960s, from The Beatles' 'Yellow Submarine' to Donovan's 'Mellow Yellow', a song that might or might not have something to do with smoking banana skins (a euphemism for hashish), although the wonderfully gauche Donovan told *NME* magazine: 'It's about being cool [and] laid-back.'

However, the phrase 'mellow yellow' has a more impressive origin – a reference to Molly Bloom's buttocks in James Joyce's magnificent *Ulysses*. Joyce's wonderfully flawed hero, Leopold Bloom, tells the world: 'I do indeed explore the plump mellow yellow smellow melons of her rump' [sic]. There is, however, no reference to 'smellow' in the Donovan version.

TIE A YELLOW RIBBON

American suffragettes were the first to wear yellow ribbons as a symbol of protest, starting in 1867, in Kansas, where yellow was the colour of the state flower – the wild sunflower. From then on it became the official colour of suffrage organizations, used for rallies, conventions and parades. They also used yellow sashes and yellow roses and during America's centennial celebrations in

An example of a yellow ribbon used to denote the cause of women's suffrage in the early twentieth century. Yellow was the colour of the movement, and can be found in posters, badges and many aspects of the symbolism women employed to further their cause.

1876 suffrage supporters sang their newly composed song, 'A Yellow Ribbon':

> Oh, we wear a yellow ribbon upon our woman's breast,
> We are prouder of its sunny hue than of a royal crest;
> 'Twas God's own primal color, born of purity and light,
> We wear it now for Liberty, for Justice and for Right.

The oldest ribbon reference comes from another song 'She Wore a Yellow Ribbon', which was brought to America by English settlers in the seventeenth century, drawing from tales relating to those waiting for a loved one to return. This was eventually recorded in 1917 under the title 'Round Her Neck She Wears a Yeller Ribbon (For Her Lover Who is Fur, Fur Away)' and it went on to become the official anthem of the US Cavalry.

A revised version of the song was used for the 1949 John Wayne film, *She Wore a Yellow Ribbon*. Another version was adopted by Arsenal Football Club, in the 1970s, and there is still a banner on the north stand at Emirates Stadium bearing the words 'She Wore a Yellow Ribbon'.

Yellow ribbons have long been displayed to welcome fighting men home. During the First World War, Canadian wives, sweethearts and mothers of soldiers used them as a sign of commitment to their loved ones. This tradition was given new life by Tony Orlando and Dawn in their 1973 hit song 'Tie a Yellow Ribbon Round the Ole Oak Tree', about a man on the bus home who has 'done his time' and wants to know if his love still wants him or will 'put the blame on me'. He sounds very much like a released criminal although the lyricist, L. Russell Brown, said he got the idea from a story about a confederate prisoner of war in Georgia, who sent a letter to his woman that he was coming home. Either way, he returns to find 'a hundred yellow ribbons round the ole oak tree'.

The song and the trope have since expanded their range. In 1983 the supporters of the Filipino exile, Benigno Aquino Jr., tied yellow ribbons around trees and played the song to welcome their leader home. However, he was assassinated, prompting the People Power revolution, the presidency of his wife, Corazon Aquino, and, in 2010, of his son, Benigno III, both of whom used yellow as their campaign colour.

In 1986 South Africa's End Conscription Campaign – an anti-apartheid protest group made up of white conscripts and their families – ran a 'tie a yellow ribbon' campaign, which inverted the homecoming tradition by tying hundreds of yellow ribbons around lampposts and trees in the major cities of the country, to focus on 'calling the troops home' and ending military conscription. One of the campaign posters extended this to schools. It read: 'Soldiers OUT of the Schools: TIE A YELLOW RIBBON AGAINST A CIVIL WAR'.

The Orlando and Dawn song was also regularly played during the 2014 pro-democracy protests in Hong Kong, where yellow ribbons were tied to street railings and used in social media as a symbol of defiance. After the police used tear gas and pepper spray on the protesters, yellow ribbons were used to oppose police

Below: An American woman decided to show her support for her husband as he fought overseas by tying a yellow ribbon and attaching a US flag to the fences lining the streets to their home. When he died she continued until the rest of his unit were back in the US safely.

WHY ARE AMERICAN TAXIS YELLOW?
John Hertz commissioned a University of Chicago survey to discover which colour would best be noticed. Yellow won. In 1914, when he started the Yellow Cab Company of Chicago, they were all painted yellow. But he wasn't the first. In 1909 orange-yellow cabs appeared in Manhattan and the Yellow Cab Company of Baltimore was founded. They spread to other cities and countries, including Canada, Australia, India, Romania, Uruguay and the Philippines.

violence. This possibly gave China the idea of using yellow ribbons to remind people of the deaths of 442 people in the sinking of the *Dong Fang Zhi Xing* cruise ship in 2015.

In Denmark, Sweden and Germany it has become an established symbol of support for troops abroad, and in Estonia there was a Facebook app for people to add a yellow ribbon to their profile pictures, in support of seven hostages held in Lebanon. In Indonesia it was a symbol of sympathy for the Indonesian Chinese victims of the 1998 riots. It has also appeared as a coming home symbol or mark of remembrance in Italy, Kuwait, Israel, South Korea and several other countries. In the US it is used to support soldiers abroad and remember those who gave their lives for their country.

The yellow ribbon has made appearances in campaigns big and small. In Australia this has ranged from the 'Save Albert Park' protest in Melbourne, where yellow ribbons were tied around trees marked for felling, to the rather more substantial appeal to support the volunteer fireman and others affected by the 2009 bushfires in Victoria, Australia. In the UK, residents of Hanwell, West London, and of Eccles, Manchester, festooned their neighbourhoods with yellow ribbons after children went missing.

Below: Yellow ribbons became a ubiquitous symbol of the protest movement in Hong Kong.

YELLOW EMPERORS

Yellow really comes into its own in China, both in the way the Chinese see the world and in the way parts of the world see the Chinese. Their five-colour system, used in philosophy, medicine, feng shui etc., has yellow at the top of the list, as the most beautiful and prestigious colour, associated with gold and wealth, with yin and yang balance and with the stabilizing energy at the centre of everything. It is the colour of glory, heroism, happiness, harmony and good luck; the colour of the yellow dragon, of the jujube and much more. It speaks of freedom from worldly cares, which is part of the reason why it is revered in Chinese Buddhism, whose monks wear yellow. It is their colour of mourning and features prominently in their temples.

Below: The mytho-historical figure of the Yellow Emperor.

Above: Ceremonies to celebrate the Yellow Emperor, considered to be the ancestor of the Chinese nation, feature participants dressed in yellow.

Chinese history is drenched in yellow. Its prominence goes back thousands of years, perhaps starting with the legend of the Yellow Emperor, also known as Gongsun Xuanyuan (2699–2588 BC), the first of five mythical yellow emperors. Additionally called the 'Yellow God of the Northern Dipper', he is said to have moulded China into a centralized state, and to have started Chinese civilization, as well as being the ancestor of all Huaxia Chinese. He is also believed to have invented just about everything of worth: writing, wheeled carts, bows and arrows. He gained his associations with yellow because the colour was said to represent the all-powerful and life-giving sun. Yellow became the colour of the rest of the first five emperors, and continued to decorate royal palaces and robes. In fact, a decree, which survived 1,400 years – from the Tang Dynasty until the twentieth-century Qing Dynasty – said that only the emperor could wear bright yellow and only his sons could wear other shades of yellow.

'YELLOW PERIL'

The word 'yellow' has frequently been used as a racist term by Americans and Europeans to describe East Asians. For example, the drifter in Bruce Springsteen's dark anti-war song, 'Born in the USA', talks of being sent to 'go and kill the yellow man' – a reference to America's failed war against the North Vietnamese. It is an enveloping term, just as 'black' includes anyone with relatively dark skin, and 'red' is used to refer to any of the Native American peoples.

The association of the East with yellow, from a Western point of view, may relate to the centrality of the colour in ancient China. Yet the world-view associated with the terms Yellow Peril and Yellow Terror, suggestive of a fear of the East, might go back in history – to the Mongol invasion of Europe led by Genghis Khan early in the thirteenth century, prompting fear of an Oriental race set on destroying Christendom, perhaps prompting a tendency to group the peoples of that area of Asia together.

Below: The Genghis Khan Monument at Zonjin Boldog, Mongolia reflects his towering presence in the history of the East and, perhaps at one time, the fears of the West.

Right: The perceived threat from China was laid bare in this poster, captioned 'The Yellow Terror in All His Glory', one of the first uses of the 'Yellow Terror' term.

Nineteenth-century European colonialism, and the arrival of Chinese migrants to America, gave renewed vigour to this racism, fanned by large doses of economic self-interest. The term 'Yellow Terror' first crops up shortly after Chinese workers migrated to California in 1870 – with white workers petitioning the authorities to block the arrival of 'filthy yellow hordes'. The lynching of around 200 Chinese men followed. A cartoon propaganda poster from this period features a ponytailed Chinese man wielding a revolver and burning stake, with a knife in his mouth, standing over his victim, a prone white woman. The caption reads, 'The Yellow Terror in All His Glory'. After this, the term moved into common parlance. For example in 1894, the *Wisconsin Daily Gazette* wrote a profile of a Chinese general, headed, 'The Yellow Terror of Oriental Wars'.

The companion term, 'Yellow Peril', can be traced to 1895 when the Hungarian General Turr, writing of the Japanese, noted that the 'yellow peril is more threatening than ever'. A few months later Kaiser Wilhelm II of Germany wrote to the Russian Tsar, Nicholas II, warning of the spectre of the Yellow Peril and the danger posed by the Great Yellow Race, by which he meant both the Chinese and the Japanese.

The Russians embraced it during the Chinese Boxer Rebellion at the turn of the twentieth century, when an alliance of nations brutally crushed an uprising. Their press used 'Yellow Peril' to depict the rebellion as a clash between 'White Holy Russia' and 'Yellow Pagan China'. The British *Daily News* picked up on the phrase in 1900, describing the Boxer Rebellion as 'the yellow peril in its most serous form' while in France the phrase was used in 1904 during the Russian-Japanese war when French newspapers wrote of the *peril jaune* (yellow peril) posed by Japanese 'barbarians'.

In the US, 'Yellow Peril' peaked in the first quarter of the twentieth century, prompting various anti-Chinese and anti-Japanese immigration acts. It waned for a while, but appeared again after the 1941 bombing of Pearl Harbor, prompting detention camps for Japanese Americans and songs such as 'When Those Little Yellow Bellies Meet the Cohens and the Kellys', 'We're Going to Find a Fellow Who is Yellow and Beat Him Red, White and Blue' and 'We're Gonna Have to Slap the Dirty Little Jap'. Fear of Mao's China later led to another revival.

Right: *Klods-Hans* magazine had a front cover in 1908 entitled 'The Western World Hopes to Defend Itself from the Asiatic Menace with Its Warships', reinforcing the distrust and fear of Asian countries, who were all grouped into one 'yellow' race by Westerners at the time.

WHAT ARE 'YELLOW-DOG DEMOCRATS'?

The term was coined in the late nineteenth century to refer to residents of the southern USA who would 'vote for a yellow dog [a term for a mongrel] before they would vote for any Republican'.

Den gule Fare

A MOUTHFUL OF YELLOW

Today all hair (and clothes) dyes are synthetic, so being a blonde has become easier than ever. Those wanting to dye clothes yellow have long had an easier and cheaper time than those desiring red or blue or black. Before the invention of synthetic dyes, the deepest, brightest and most expensive yellow came from hand-picked saffron. There were several cheaper alternatives, though, which still produced an acceptable yellow, including yellow ochre, turmeric and jackfruit juice.

Paints, however, presented a problem in the past. One option was Indian Yellow oil paint, pigmented with the crystallized urine of cows, or water buffalo, fed exclusively on mango leaves, which made them suffer. It stank, but was still widely used until 1910. A noted artist who used and was said to admire Indian Yellow was J. M. W. Turner.

Several alternative yellow pigments were highly toxic, including chrome yellow, made from lead-chromium oxide. When mixed with acid it turned a brilliant yellow; when mixed with alkali it turned orange, but it contained high levels of poisonous lead. The Dutch painter Vincent van Gogh was particularly fond of chrome yellow – which he used in painting his famous sunflowers, yellow calendulas, stars and lamplight. During a psychotic episode towards the end of his short life, there was evidence he squeezed yellow paint directly from the tube into his mouth. If true, this would have caused lead poisoning, which can prompt aggressive behaviour, confusion, memory loss, insomnia and fatigue, along with physical problems. In other words, it could have exacerbated the mental condition that led to his suicide. At a push, it could be that van Gogh's love of yellow finally killed him.

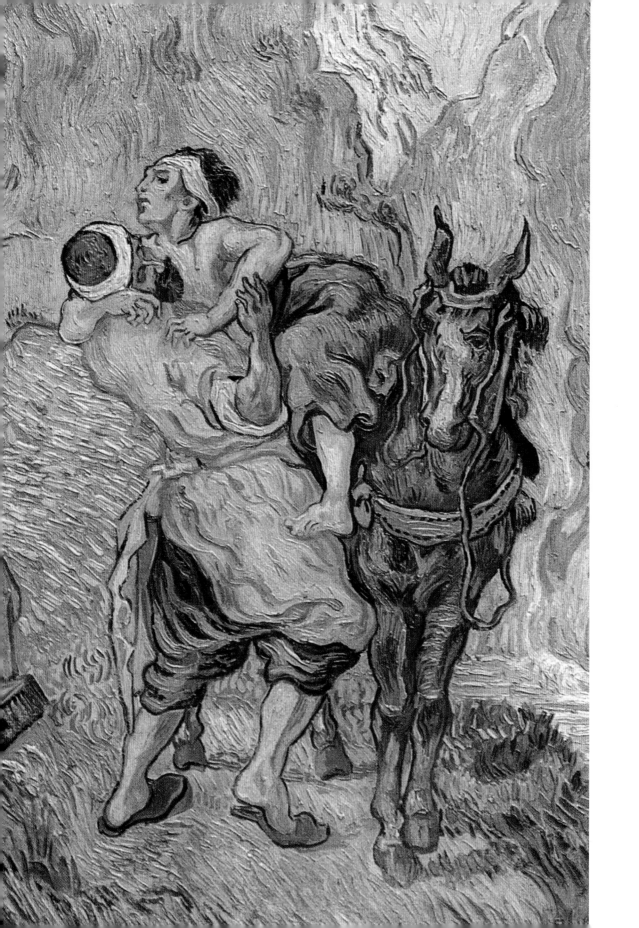

YELLOWING UP

Another expression of 'yellow' prejudice came through Hollywood's depiction of 'Orientals', which led to the phrase 'yellowing up' (drawn from 'blacking up'), where white actors would give stereotypical portrayals of Chinese or Japanese people. The most persistent came through various versions of the evil, criminal Chinese genius Dr Fu Manchu, starting with Arthur Hughes in 1929, followed by Boris Karloff, Christopher Lee and others, and ending with Peter Sellers in 1980 – and a later comical version by Nicolas Cage in 1987 in *Werewolf Women of the SS*. All twelve actors who played Fu Manchu were white. But the most insensitive example of 'yellow face' came with the 1961 film *Breakfast at Tiffany's*, where the director Blake Edwards instructed a heavily made-up Mickey Rooney to ham it up as Holly Golightly's ridiculous, buck-toothed, myopic Japanese neighbour I. Y. Yunioshi.

Left: Christopher Lee, the English actor, as Fu Manchu.

Previous page: Van Gogh's love of yellow was evident in much of his work, including *The Good Samaritan*, reproduced here.

THE YELLOW PRESS

Above: An early depiction of the Yellow Kid.

The press was deemed yellow because of a battle between Pulitzer's *New York World* and Hearst's *New York Journal* in the 1890s. Pulitzer published a cartoon called *The Yellow Kid*, printed in yellow ink, but Hearst poached his cartoonist. The incensed Pulitzer hired another cartoonist to continue the cartoon. This battle prompted the *New York Press* editor, Erwin Wardman, to refer to the 'school of yellow-kid journalism' and then to 'yellow journalism'. The name stuck and was applied to papers like Hearst's and Pulitzer's, specializing in half-truths, sensational headlines and lacking properly researched news.

WHY WERE YELLOW BOOKS RISQUÉ?

During the second half of the nineteenth century, French novels considered anti-establishment, risqué and decadent were often bound in yellow covers as a way of branding and marketing them. In Oscar Wilde's *The Picture of Dorian Gray*, the eponymous Dorian is first corrupted by reading a yellow book. This prompted two British publishers to name their illustrated quarterly literary periodical *The Yellow Book*, because many of its articles and stories fell into the Victorian view of 'aestheticism' and 'decadence'. When Wilde was arrested for sodomy in 1895, local newspaper headlines said he was carrying a 'yellow book' and a stone-throwing mob responded by attacking the offices of the periodical, although he was not carrying a copy of *The Yellow Book* but rather a yellow-covered French novel, *Aphrodite*, by Pierre Louys.

GREEN

GREEN IS USUALLY the most benign of colours. The word itself comes from the Anglo-Saxon *growan*, which means 'to grow' and it evokes images of verdant grass, herbs, shrubs and trees.

Today green is the colour of serenity and peacefulness, the safe-to-go colour of traffic lights, and has been chosen as the colour of the environmental movement and the political parties it spawned. It is also the colour of Gaelic Ireland, drawn from the tale of the green shamrock of Saint Patrick, used to denote the Holy Trinity. In pre-colonial, Central and South America, green symbolized fertility. For the Aztecs the rich iridescent green plumage of the quetzal bird was a sign of abundance. The Egyptian hieroglyphic symbol for green was the green stalk of the papyrus, and it is to growth and, by extension, life, that green will always return.

Green belongs to a kind of countryside nostalgia for simpler times that has been a trope in high and low culture over the last two centuries, ever since the start of the Industrial Revolution, contrasting the contemporaneous grey with the verdant rural idyll of days gone by.

This is reflected in the arts, from William Wordsworth, who wrote poems that romanticized the greenery of nature, to Richard Llewellyn, who wrote his 1939 novel *How Green Was My Valley*, which was made into a film in 1941, about the Welsh coalfields replacing the rural valleys. The 1965 Porter Wagoner song, 'Green, Green Grass of Home' (which also became a Tom Jones hit), tells the story of a man waking up on death row after a dream of the green fields and trees of home, where he will soon be buried.

As with all colours, green's associations do not all head in the same direction. Green is the colour of inexperience, drawn from the freshness of greenery in nature: 'green behind the ears', or simply 'green'. Green's literal associations are not restricted to sprouting shoots and lush valleys. For example, when dead flesh rots, it can become greenish in colour. Although gangrene can turn flesh greenish, the word 'gangrene' has nothing to do with green – it comes from the Greek word meaning 'to devour'. The term 'green around the gills', which emerged in the middle of the nineteenth century, comes from the pallid greenish skin of people who are about to vomit, as the colour drains from the face.

SAINT PATRICK
AND GREEN

Saint Patrick, the fifth-century priest who became a saint in the seventh century, arrived in Ireland (from England) as a slave, before escaping six years later. He returned to England, entered the priesthood, and was sent back to Ireland, but this time as a missionary, and a remarkably successful one at that.

One of his methods was to use the three-leafed shamrock to teach the locals about the Holy Trinity: the father, the son and the Holy Spirit. The symbol of the shamrock gave rise to

Right: Saint Patrick holding the shamrock, each leaf representing a member of the Holy Trinity.

green as the colour of the Irish nation, particularly after the Protestants adopted orange as their colour. Soon, green had become synonymous with Irish identity. For example, the pro-independence Irish Home Rule movement flew a flag with a golden harp on a green background.

THE GREEN-EYED MONSTER

The most common of all green's negative associations has nothing to do with greenery or ailing flesh. Thanks to William Shakespeare, for more than 400 years green has been the colour of envy and jealousy, at least in the English-speaking world – the French prefer yellow, the Chinese red, the Japanese purple, the Finns black. It starts with *Othello*, written in 1603. The villain, Iago, plots to make Othello jealous of his wife, Desdemona, and warns him:

> O, beware, my lord, of jealousy!
> It is the green-ey'd monster, which doth mock
> The meat it feeds on

Two years later Shakespeare reused the phrase, this time through the mouth of his heroine Portia who, in *The Merchant of Venice*, says:

> How all the other passions fleet to air
> As doubtful thoughts, and rash-embraced despair,
> And shuddering fear, and green-eyed jealousy!
> O love, be moderate. Allay thy ecstasy.

Shakespeare likens the emotion of jealousy to a disease that eats away at the person, which is why he describes it as a green-eyed monster that feeds on meat and causes fear.

GREEN KNIGHTS AND MERRY MEN

European mythology is rich with greens, no doubt because so many of the stories are bound up with the natural world. Fairies were often portrayed wearing green, sometimes with green wings, and usually in a green forest setting. A few even had green skin, prompting the nickname of the potent alcoholic French spirit absinthe, which is known as *La Fée Verte* (the Green Fairy).

English literature's most famous fairies and elves – William Shakespeare's Puck and J. M. Barrie's Peter Pan – are invariably dressed in green. In one of the most resilient of modern-day fairy tales, Dorothy's quest ends in the Emerald City where the Wizard of Oz wears green and the Wicked Witch of the West is green, at least in the 1939 film.

Below: Puck in Shakespeare's *A Midsummer's Night Dream* (left), and J. M. Barrie's Peter Pan (right), their greens revealing their connections to the natural world.

There are good green mythical creatures and bad ones. Take, for instance, one of the great texts of Middle English, *Sir Gawain and the Green Knight*, written in the late 1300s, but drawing on older European folklore about the Green Man story. The idea of a gigantic green knight – with green hair and beard, 'as green as green could be', wearing green clothes, riding a green horse, carrying a green and gold axe and a holly branch – has resonance in the mythology of several continents. Green men, tied to nature but with super powers of their own, pop up all over the place in legend, sculpture and stone carving, all related to themes of rebirth and of the growth cycle that begins each spring.

In the Green Knight story, Sir Gawain, youngest of King Arthur's knights of the round table, accepts a challenge from the Green Knight, who arrives at the New Year's feast. Gawain agrees to strike the imposter with an axe blow to win the knight's own magnificent axe, on condition that, in a year and a day, he receives a return blow. Gawain beheads the Green Knight with a single blow, after which the giant retrieves his head and reminds Gawain of his bargain. Gawain goes to keep his side of the deal but, wearing a green and gold girdle made by a sorceress, he believes he'll be protected from harm. He is indeed barely harmed by the Green Knight, but not because of the girdle. Rather, it is because the Green Knight turns out to be the noble Bertilak, the lord of the castle Gawain is staying at, magically transformed, who was merely testing the young knight's resolve. Gawain returns to Camelot, still wearing the girdle as a symbol of his deceit and cowardice. His fellow knights absolve him of blame and decide they will all wear green baldrics (sword belts) as a reminder to stay honest.

Rivalling the Arthurian legend is the tale of Robin Hood, whose popularity owes much to its theme of stealing from the rich and giving to the poor. He is also famous for clothing himself and his Merry Men in Lincoln green. The story might, or might not,

WHAT IS THE GREEN LANGUAGE?

In the mythology of several parts of the world, the language of birds and beasts (and sometimes of gods) is known as the 'green language', and those mystics with the supposed power to understand it were seen as particularly wise (although this could also be acquired through a taste of dragon blood). In the Qur'an and the Talmud the wise Solomon/Suleiman was taught the language of the birds and beasts by God, as was his father, David, in the Islamic version.

have emerged from the exploits of a real-life Nottinghamshire outlaw called Robert Hod, who failed to appear in court in 1225. Or, alternatively, from a 1261 outlaw called William Robehod. Whatever the origin, legend grew to the point where fugitives from justice became known as 'Robin Hoods'.

More than a century later there is an account of a priest complaining that his parishioners preferred hearing 'a tale or song of Robyn Hood' to listening to a sermon, suggesting its renown even then. Robin Hood emerges in medieval English literature in 'Piers Plowman', a 1375 poem, and his story grows through fifteenth- and sixteenth-century ballads. The reigning king changes from Edward to Richard the Lionheart, while Robin evolves from yeoman to nobleman and new characters like Maid Marian and Friar Tuck are introduced. There are Robin Hood references in four Shakespeare plays, by which time the story is more or less set, demonstrating the popularity of the legend: Robin fights for the poor under the regency of John and his henchmen, as England waits for King Richard to return from his crusade. This is shown in the stained-glass window image overleaf, which depicts the history of Robin Hood.

The earliest reference to Lincoln green came in 1510, in a version of the Robin Hood story that states: 'when they were clothed in Lyncolne grene they kest away their gray'.

Lincoln was a town well known for its cloth industry in the Middle Ages, and specialized in woollen cloths dyed with woad blue. Lincoln green was achieved by re-dyeing the blue cloth with weld yellow. The Lincoln dyers also produced red cloth, by using the ground bodies of the kermes scale insect from the Mediterranean. This may explain the clothing of Hood's compatriot Will Scarlet. In fact, one version of the legend has Robin wearing scarlet too, while his Merry Men wear green. Scarlet cloth would have been very expensive compared with green, for which the woad and weld plants grow wild in Britain.

In other parts of Europe different recipes were used to make green. For example, a fourteenth-century German recipe issues the following instructions: 'To make a green dye, take verdigris and boil it in urine and mix alum thereto and a portion of gum arabic, and dye therewith.'

Previous page: The earliest illustration of the story of Sir Gawain and the Green Knight, fourteenth century. The top part of the work shows King Arthur granting Gawain his boon, with Queen Guinevere and a courtier with a curved sword also present.

Right: Robin Hood and his Merry Men, dressed in Lincoln green.

Following page: A stained-glass window depicts the history of Robin Hood.

THE GRASS IS
ALWAYS GREENER

Similar to the green-eyed monster of envy, 'the grass is always greener' is a phrase used when someone feels that others are getting a better deal in life – that your own life will be improved if only you make a change to something that seems preferable at the time. For example, in the fairy tale the 'Three Billy Goats Gruff', as the three goats want to cross the bridge to reach the greener grass on the other side of the river. They are foolish enough to risk their lives attempting to cross the bridge, rather than settling for what they already have.

It has prompted the cautionary proverb, 'the grass is always greener on the other side of the fence', used to suggest someone is being dazzled by the illusion that others have it better or that a different life will be superior.

It seems that the concept has existed for some time. The *Oxford Dictionary of Proverbs* suggested it might be drawn from the Latin proverb *Fertilior seges est alieno semper in arvo*, which was cited by Erasmus of Rotterdam and then translated into English in 1545 as 'The corne in an other mans ground semeth euer more fertyll and plentifull then doth oure owne' [sic]. To translate this into modern English: The corn in another man's field always seems more fertile and plentiful than one's own.

There are several variations of the proverb: 'Hills look green far away' (first recorded in literature in 1887), 'The grass is always greener in the other fellow's yard' (1924 American song), 'Distant pastures always look greener' (first recorded in 1936) and 'The grass is greener on the other side of the hedge' (first recorded in 1959). A related proverb is: 'The apples on the other side of the wall are the sweetest'.

Inevitably, other countries have their own versions of the 'grass is greener' proverb, too, because coveting other people's lives and possessions is a common part of the human condition. In Japanese the proverb is identical, and in Indonesian the phrase is 'The neighbour's grass always looks more green'. The Roman poet Ovid wrote in his *Art of Love*: 'The harvest is always richer in the other man's field.'

It has certainly become a clichéd staple of popular culture. One example is the 1963 New Christy Minstrels hit song, 'Green, Green', in which the chorus tells of going away 'to where the grass is greener still'.

RELIGIOUS GREEN

Green beats blue as the colour of choice for those who believe in a god or gods, which relates to associations with rebirth. Modern humans have shown signs of religious ritual for at least 60,000 years, but the first green god that we know of comes rather later – about 4,500 years ago – with the green-skinned Egyptian god of the afterlife, Osiris, who was sometimes said to be the eldest son of the earth god Geb.

Another, from the Tibetan Buddhist tradition, is the eleventh-century yogi and mystic Jetsun Milarepa, who is often depicted as having a greenish hue – they say he survived on nettle tea, after abandoning his black magic ways, which turned his skin green.

Below: Green-skinned Osiris with the pharoah Seti I.

Christianity and Judaism also have their share of green in their founding mythology through 'God's garden' – later known as the 'Garden of Eden' – which probably drew its inspiration from the Babylonian legend of a primordial man placed in a divine garden to guard the tree of life. It is also similar to the garden of the Hesperides in Greek mythology. In each of these stories, the garden is described as a lush, rich, fertile green, as are the various versions of paradise.

Islam puts all the other religions in the shade when it comes to its devotion to green. The colour is associated with creation, the Garden of Eden, paradise, resurrection and with the Prophet Muhammad himself – he wears green, white, or both, including a green turban.

Green turbans were also worn by his successors and the green associations of paradise in the Qur'an are more specific than with other religions, with mention of green robes, green silk couches and the green eternal garden, where Allah welcomes martyred souls, who fly his way in the form of green birds. It is no wonder that so many mosques, all over the world, have green domes (see the mosque in Muscat, Oman below), or that so many flags from Islamic countries have green as the dominant colour, going back to their use of green in banners at the time of the Fatimid Caliphate.

A key figure in the Islamic tradition is the prophet al-Khidr – The Green One – who is described in the Qur'an as a wise and righteous servant and messenger of God who travelled with Moses. He is portrayed wearing a green cloak and turban. Muhammad tells his companions that the reason al-Khidr is called 'The Green One' is because when he sits on the barren ground, green shoots appear: in other words, he brings life.

In Sufi Islam, The Green One has immortality and is said to appear to them anonymously, hinting at his identity by sometimes wearing green. For Sufis, choosing 'the green death' means giving up your beautiful clothes and instead wearing patched, discarded and worthless rags. One's life then becomes 'green' because of the 'verdant grace' one has chosen. Green is also the dynastic colour of the Shiites and, as a result, is particularly popular in Shiite iconography.

One result of the Islamic fondness for green was that the colour became viewed unfavourably by the Christian crusaders. It came to be associated with devils and demons (below), and in the theatre those wearing green would meet with a nasty end. This started at the time of the crusades in the twelfth century and the association between green and bad luck lingered in France and other parts of Europe until at least the early nineteenth century.

DEATHLY GREEN

In 1775 a Swedish chemist, Carl Wilhelm Scheele, invented a new pea-green pigment he called Scheele's green. It soon became extremely popular in paints and as a dye, used for carpets, candles, fabrics of various kinds, ballroom gowns, wallpaper and confectionery. A story in *The Times* in 1863 estimated that more than 500 tons of Scheele's green was being produced annually in Britain alone to feed this demand.

However, the pigment contained copper arsenite as its key ingredient, which was toxic and could cause cancer and a range of other ailments. If conditions were dry, then tiny particles of arsenic became airborne. When it was humid or damp, a mould would form, giving off a mousy smell and releasing even larger doses of poison into the air. Children and old people were particularly susceptible, and many became ill and died in their rooms.

In 1814 a new version came on to the market, known as Emerald green, delighting users because of its brighter tones. But this too was laced with arsenic. In one notable case in 1860, a chef used it to colour his gourmet blancmange for a London society dinner. Three of his diners died from arsenic poisoning. In another case, a girl died after licking off the green coating on an artificial bunch of grapes.

The following year, the toxicity of arsenic was scientifically detected and warnings were issued. The *British Medical Journal* wrote, in 1871, that a six-inch sample of Scheele's green wallpaper contained enough arsenic to kill two people, and that this wallpaper could be found just about everywhere, 'from the palace down to the navvy's hut'. One might wonder what took the authorities so long, especially as arsenic was popular as a potent rat poison. In fact, eighty-three years earlier Scheele had written to a friend, saying that he wasn't sure whether to warn users that his pigment was toxic. He decided not to, as it would have been bad for business. Despite the revelation of its toxicity, Scheele's green wasn't banned because the industry was so large. It took another four decades before manufacturers stopped making it and consumers stopped buying it.

Below: Scheele's service to green was commemorated with this green Swedish postage stamp.

A DICTATOR'S
GREEN DEATH?

Napoleon Bonaparte died in exile on the island of St Helena in 1821, at the age of fifty-one. The official cause of death was stomach cancer, which had also killed his father, but for many years it was thought he may have been poisoned with arsenic, due to his symptoms. His British captors were suspected, but it may have been the wallpaper in his humid bedroom, later found to contain Scheele's green.

In 2007 one of his hairs was tested by Italy's National Institute of Nuclear Physics, confirming the presence of arsenic. Although his arsenic level was 100 times higher than the current average, it

Below: *The Death of Napoleon* by Charles de Steuben – but did Scheele's green hasten the former ruler's end?

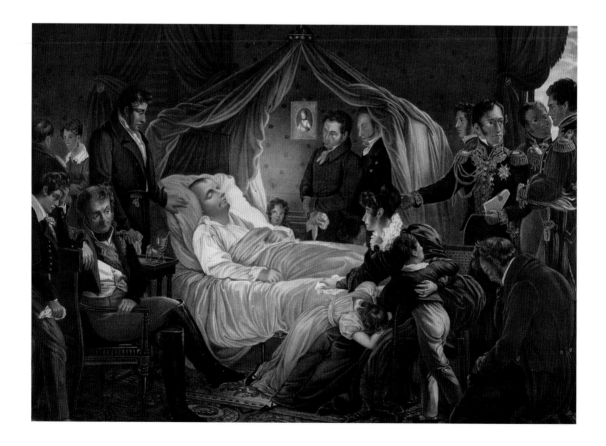

wasn't actually much higher than the average for people of his class and time, who were frequently exposed to arsenic through dyes and paints. Later tests of hairs preserved from earlier in his life showed similarly high arsenic levels. So the wallpaper probably didn't kill him, though it may have speeded his demise. Now it is believed that the cause of death was indeed bowel cancer, plus a perforated ulcer.

LITTLE GREEN MEN

The concept of aliens being little green men began with the 1955 'Kelly-Hopkinsville sighting'. Two Kentucky farmers claimed their farmhouse had been attacked by aliens from a spaceship, but they drove them off with gunfire. The metallic silver aliens were said to be less than four feet tall with large pointed ears, claw-like hands and glowing yellow eyes. There was no mention of green, but it was added by some newspapers to make the story more appealing.

In England, the mystical 'green children of Woolpit' appeared to twelfth-century villagers. The earliest US reference comes from an 1899 story in the *Atlanta Constitution* about a green-skinned alien from Mars. *Tarzan* author Edgar Rice Burroughs wrote a story in 1912 about twelve-foot-tall 'green men of Mars'. But it was only after Kelly-Hopkinsville that 'little green men' became part of popular parlance.

Following page: Fairies – so often depicted in green because of their association with nature – and their supposedly wanton behaviour saw the colour green take on a more negative light in western Europe.

WHY DO SURGEONS WEAR GREEN SCRUBS?

Surgeons used to operate in their suits, then, with awareness of the importance of cleanliness, they began to wear white aprons. However, this displayed the blood more vividly than any colour, so they left operating theatres looking like butchers. In addition, they found that the contrasting colours of red and white were distracting and tiring to the eye. The solution was blue-green 'scrubs', because blue-green is the complementary colour of red, making the blood less visible and preventing optical strain.

MARRIED IN GREEN

A 1949 American marriage etiquette book advises: 'Green typifies youth, hope and happiness.' This is the opposite of the Scottish and northern English tradition. For example, a nineteenth-century rhyme on wedding colours includes the advice: 'Married in green, ashamed to be seen.' An earlier version goes: 'Married in green, not fit to be seen.' In the English midlands it was once the colour associated with being abandoned, prompting the ditty: 'Green and white / Forsaken quite.' Writing in 1866 on the folklore of northern England, William Henderson advised: 'Green, ever an ominous colour in the lowlands of Scotland, must on no account be worn there at a wedding … In fact nothing green must make its appearance that day; kale and all other green vegetables are excluded from the wedding dinner.' There was one Scottish exception, however – the tradition of unmarried elder sisters having to don green stockings or garters at the weddings of younger sisters – a symbol of their shame.

This association with bad luck might have come from green fairies – if one has the temerity to choose the fairies' colour, one is in for a hard time. Fairies were also thought to be sexually wanton, and so it was that green became a colour of promiscuity in western Europe. The phrase 'to give one a green gown' was a euphemism for permitting coitus. It goes back to at least the 1600s. For example, Robert Herrick writes in his poem 'Corinna's Gone A-Maying': 'Many a green-gown has been given / Many a kiss, both odd and even'.

BLUE

YOU MIGHT THINK blue and green are distinct colours. The leaves and grass are green; the sky and sea are blue. They don't look alike. But actually, in some cultures, they do. Blue is a relatively recent addition to the colour chart and doesn't exist in several parts of the world. It was only in the eleventh century that it came into its own in English.

Perhaps this had something to do with nature – the sky is simply the sky, the sea is simply the sea (and both change their colours frequently). For the rest, nature is pretty sparing in its production of blues (we tend to get stuck after blueberries, bluebirds, bluebottles, blue-finned tunny and bluebells, which are really closer to violet). It also has to do with the historical shortage of blue dyes and pigments – unknown in rock art, and hard to come by in the millennia that followed.

THE BLUE-GREEN CONUNDRUM

In most contemporary European languages the etymology of the word 'blue' begins with either black or green, rather than from any blue thing in life. The ancient Egyptians were fond of blue, and had their own word for it, whereas the Chinese, Japanese and Hebrews did not. Indeed, they may not have seen it as a colour at all. For the Ancient Greeks blue was merely a variant of green without a name of its own. *The Odyssey* by Homer had not a single reference to blue, but hundreds of mentions of black and white and other murkier shades. He talks of the 'wine-dark sea' but never the blue sea.

When the reforming British prime minister, William Gladstone, who studied Ancient Greek in his spare time, discovered that Homer lacked a word for blue, he speculated that the Greeks must have been colour-blind. What Gladstone hadn't realized

The Egyptians having a term for the colour blue was likely in part because of their access to lapis lazuli and its use in their art.

was that this linguistic colour-blindness was not restricted to the Ancient Greeks – as well as Chinese, Japanese and Hebrew, the Hindu Vedic hymns are full of colourful references to the heavens, but blue is again the one colour missing. It was, in fact, the last of the primary colours to be identified by the ancients. And when all of the languages of the world are considered, identification of blue as a unique colour comes later than black, white, red, yellow or green, on average. Several modern languages have similar blue-green blurring, including Zulu, Korean, Vietnamese, Thai and Kurdish.

One reason for what we might consider to be the confusion between blue and green is that they are part of a continuum in the colour spectrum, so some people fail to see much difference. But in some cultures different factors come into play when specifying colours. For example, for the Mota people of the Banks Islands, in the Pacific, colour description relates to shininess, tone and texture. A shiny version of a colour will be given a different name from a matte version but a green leaf is the same colour as the blue sky.

A people who have recently attracted attention for their green-blue differentiation are the Himba tribe of Namibia, a 50,000-strong semi-nomadic people who live near the Angolan border. Westerners have many names and descriptions of colours, while the Himba have just four – *zoozu* (most dark colours, greens, blues, reds and purples); *vapa* (white and some yellows);

borou (other shades of green and blue); and *dumbu* (other shades of green, and reds and browns).

A few years ago, the BBC screened a programme on colour perception involving the Himba. In one test, members of the tribe were given a number of green squares and one blue square to identify. They had trouble making the distinction. Then they were given a number of green squares, one of which was in a different shade of green. They had no trouble with this one, whereas Western volunteers struggled. The Himba's reason for having unusual group categories for colours is that they relate to hunting conditions: daylight, sunlight, dusk and evening. As a result, they have difficulty telling colours apart, such as blue and green, but are very good at judging different tones of colour. So, like the Ancient Greeks, the Himba have no word for blue, because they have never needed one. It seems that, when it comes to colour, language influences perception.

Above is the coloured-square test the Himba both excelled at and struggled with. Can you identify which square is a different shade of green?

TURQUOISE

Colour specialists say that turquoise is 70 per cent blue and 30 per cent green. The name, incidentally, is drawn from the semi-precious gem rather than the other way around (the word came from the Turkish source of the gems and made its way into English in the late sixteenth century). Today turquoise, like all colours, is sub-divided: celeste, turquoise blue, light turquoise, medium turquoise, dark turquoise, pearl mystic turquoise. In contemporary fashion, it is these days mainly pushed as a feminine colour.

English speakers split blue into two, like Russian does, for example. Instead, they use qualifying adjectives, such as dark blue, light blue, pale blue, baby blue, navy blue, icy blue, sky blue. In contrast, red is accompanied by pink, rather than light red or pale red, because pink is regarded as a different colour from red.

THE BLUES

The origin of the phrase 'feeling blue' is sometimes said to be nautical. One claim is that it all started in the days of ocean-going sailing ships – when the captain or an officer died during the voyage, blue flags would be flown and the hull was daubed with a blue-painted line after the ship docked.

It may also allude to the dead appearing bluish or, indeed, the colour of skin when cold, wet and tired, so that feeling blue is a metaphor for feeling uncomfortable and miserable – fed up with one's lot in life.

This leads us to the call-and-response, guitar-based songs that arose from the music of former slaves in America, drawing from West African roots. What we now know as 'the blues' goes back to the end of the nineteenth century: the secular music of poor black people, with the lyrics telling stories of the singer's woes in a harsh and unforgiving world – bad cops, brutal prisons, white oppression, unfaithful lovers, violent lovers, unrequited love, unwanted pregnancies, floods, drought, gambling, devils, hard times.

When this music first emerged, the term 'feeling blue' already featured strongly in popular American parlance, and calling this new musical form 'the blues' seemed to fit. So it was that the motif of blue, which started with the blues, found its way into related musical forms – from Miles Davis's signature collection *Kind of Blue* and John Coltrane's *Blue Train*, to Joni Mitchell's breakthrough album of confessional songs, *Blue*, Madonna's *True Blue* and Massive Attack's *Blue Lines*, and so many more.

THE WORLD'S FAVOURITE COLOUR

The other side of blue's connotations of sadness is that in most cultures it is also associated with cooling and calming. Students given IQ tests with blue covers are said to have an edge of a few points over those given tests with red covers. The former is seen as calming, the latter as agitating. It could be that this has something to do with some inherent properties in the two colours relating to the way the brain absorbs the wavelengths of the light when it reflects off the molecules of a blue surface, but it could also relate to blue's cooling ecological associations – seas, lakes, rivers, skies – while red suggests danger and blood.

Despite its associations with sadness, hard times and depression, colour tests in several cultures have found that blue is the world's favourite colour – in one study of colour preference in ten countries, blue came out on top in all of them, and was way ahead of any other colour. This applies to women and girls as well as men and boys, and yet, in the West, in recent years we've come to think of blue as a masculine colour. As we shall see when we look at the feminine connotations of pink, there's nothing inherent in this.

Which one of the colours listed below do you like the most?

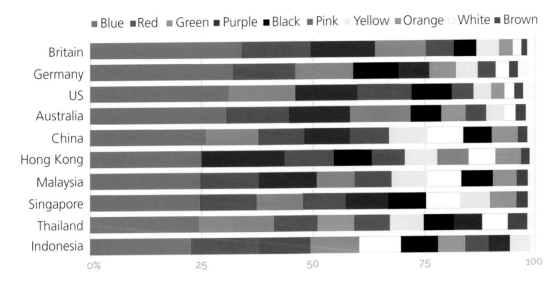

Rich Romans in the Western Empire came to despise blue, seeing it as an effeminate colour for men, and in modern Russia gay men are called 'sky blues'. In some Catholic countries in Europe, blue was seen as feminine because of its association with the Virgin Mary. Beyond the Catholic world, blue was frequently cited as a girls' colour in early twentieth-century magazines, with mothers advised to dress their girls in blue if they wanted them to grow up feminine.

RELIGIOUS BLUES

When it comes to religious worship, blue comes after green as the colour of choice. In Catholic Christianity, much of this involves Marian worship – the Virgin Mary was invariably portrayed as wearing a blue mantle. In reality, a woman of the lowly status

of the Mary of the Gospels, in first-century Palestine, would have worn colourless clothes of natural wool. Dyes were expensive and some colours were reserved for the rich, the powerful and the Romans. Mary's blue mantle therefore wasn't in the minds of the early Christians – it first appeared in the sixth century AD in Byzantium. Catholic sources offer various related reasons: it was the colour worn by an empress; it was the colour of peace and tranquillity; it was the colour of heaven and earth.

Catholicism wasn't the only religious persuasion to favour blue. The Hindu god Lord Vishnu, who is said to be the preserver of the world, and is associated with water, and the compassionate Rama, seventh avatar of Vishnu, are both usually portrayed with blue skins, while the Hindu destroyer god, Shiva, is also depicted in blue and is called 'blue-throated' because he swallowed poison to win the battle between the gods and the demons. Buddhists use turquoise-blue prayer beads and the Mongol Buddha of the East, Akshobhya, was portrayed in blue because, to his followers, the colour was suggestive of his power to destroy enemies.

Above: The Virgin Mary in her blue robe, a colour, historically speaking, that it is unlikely she would have been able to afford, given her probable lack of wealth.

Above: Vishnu, Krishna (top), Rama and Shiva (bottom) are all portrayed as blue-skinned.

In Exodus, there's an account of Moses and his men ascending Mount Sinai after the Jewish people had ratified the Covenant, after which God decided to impress them with a show of his majesty. According to Exodus 24:10: 'Under his feet was something like a pavement made of lapis lazuli.' The Jewish Talmud and Mishnah teach that the Ten Commandment tablets were made of blue sapphire, so that Moses could point to the heavens and to God's throne. Orthodox Jewish prayer shawls have blue bands near the edges, the idea being that the pure colour of sky draws them into thinking deeper about God. However, no one can be sure what kind of sky God or the writers of the Torah had in mind when using the Hebrew word for blue dye, *Tekhelet*, because the fiercely guarded instructions were lost in the sacking of Jerusalem and the destruction of the second temple in AD 70. Various commentators have described it as resembling the noonday sky (*Maimonides*), the evening sky (*Rashi*), the blue of sapphires and even the colour green. The modern makers of prayer shawls have settled for sky blue.

BLUE BLOOD

Religion, or religious fanaticism, along with xenophobia, is also the source of the term 'blue blood', for anyone with aristocratic pretensions. Until 1492 Jews, Muslims and Christians rubbed along just fine in Muslim-ruled Spanish Granada. Then the Christians under Ferdinand of Aragon and Isabella of Castille conquered this last outpost of Islamic Spain and introduced the Spanish Inquisition, which meant that Jews and Muslims were forced to flee or to convert.

Those who stayed were darker-skinned people of North African descent, while their new overlords were lighter-skinned, which meant their blue veins could be seen in their necks and arms. One way of proving your Christian credentials was to show your 'blue blood'. It all began in Spain but soon other class-obsessed Europeans picked up on it – those with aristocratic links were referred to as 'blue bloods', in reference to their supposed nobility.

BLUE ART

The relentless search for 'true' blue paint to portray the Virgin Mary was carried out with as much fervour and frustration as the search for red dye. Artists like Leonardo da Vinci made sure they got the best pigments for their versions of the Virgin, which meant breaking the bank for precious ultramarine blue paint made from lapis lazuli, imported from Afghanistan, although others used cheaper and less brilliant blues made from azurite, which even Leonardo used to depict Judas. Lapis lazuli had a long pedigree – used for ancient Afghan ceramics, Mesopotamian sculpture, Egyptian jewellery, Roman aphrodisiacs and the elaborate capital letters of medieval manuscript illuminations.

Using lapis lazuli to make paint involved grinding the mineral into an extremely fine powder, which was a laborious and expensive process, even if one could afford the lapis lazuli in the first place. This all changed in the early 1700s with the chance discovery of Prussian blue, through mixing iron sulphate and potash, which was far cheaper and didn't fade.

Despite the increased availability of blue paint, one of England's leading eighteenth-century artists, Joshua Reynolds, said that a true artist would never use blue as the centrepiece of any painting. It was too cold for that, and was best used for background and

Below: Lapis lazuli was used in everything from Egyptian art to illuminated manuscripts.

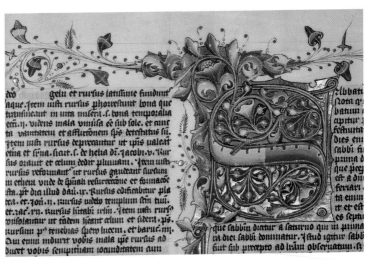

shadows. Thomas Gainsborough took him up on this and painted what would become one of his most famous pictures, *The Blue Boy*, in 1770, featuring a boy dressed entirely in blue.

After the late nineteenth century most paints and dyes were synthetic so there was no shortage of blues in whatever shade was desired, and some artists became known for favouring the colour – Pablo Picasso's 'Blue Period' during the first few years of the twentieth century is perhaps the most celebrated today. But no one has embraced blue more than the New York-based conceptual photographer Spencer Tunick. To celebrate the maritime heritage of the English town of Hull, he persuaded more than 3,000 locals to turn up naked, after which they were painted top to tail in four shades of blue. They then posed around some of the city's historical places and were photographed for a project he dubbed *Sea of Hull*.

French artist Yves Klein had 'International Klein blue' named after him, as he devoted his artistic life to developing the purest blue possible. He had painted almost 200 IKB works by his death in 1962, each a canvas painted entirely in his blue.

WHY ARE INTELLECTUAL WOMEN CALLED 'BLUESTOCKINGS'?

It goes back to the late seventeenth century, with the term initially describing men wearing cheaper and more informal blue worsted stockings rather than more formal black silk ones. In the mid-eighteenth century blue-stockinged men and women frequented literary gatherings organized by a trio of prominent society women, which became known as the Blue Stockings Society. These well-read women were referred to as the 'blue-stocking ladies'.

BLUE EYES

In Islam blue is seen as one of the essential colours of nature, representing water and the sky and it can be seen in blue mosques all over the Muslim world. But it also has negative associations. The Qur'an (Surah Taha 102 v 20) reads: 'The day when the trumpet is blown; and We shall gather the guilty, blue-eyed on that day'. This suggestion that the blue-eyed were to be damned on the day of judgement contributed to a widespread view that blue-eyed people were not to be trusted, one that has roots in pre-Islamic Arab thought. In parts of the Muslim world, the negative associations of blue persist. For instance, Palestinians and Syrians might talk of someone whose 'bones are blue', meaning he is no good.

Previous page: Spencer Tunick's *Sea of Hull* saw 3,000 naked locals painted in four shades of blue.

Below: Blue is a prominent colour in some mosque designs. The stunning Sheikh Lotfollah Mosque in Isfahan, Iran, catching the late afternoon sunlight, is a particularly impressive example.

Above: Turkish amulets, displayed for sale on this tree, bear blue eyes to protect their wearers from harm.

This unease about blue eyes was also found in non-Islamic parts of Central Asia where a blue-eyed person was considered to be of dubious character – and to be ugly. It is likely that this prejudice had something to do with the scarcity of blue eyes in that part of the world – and its association with outsiders and colonists. In Turkey, however, many people wear an amulet with a blue eye to protect them from the 'Evil Eye'.

Originally, all people had brown eyes. Blue eyes, which have low levels of melanin (also the determiner of skin colour), evolved long after African people migrated to the colder climates of Europe. It is now thought that a single genetic mutation prompted the recessive trait for blue eyes – and that they first emerged in the north-western Black Sea region, probably less than 10,000 years ago. Precisely when is not known, but it seems they may have evolved before 'white' skin.

Today, blue eyes are most common in northern and eastern Europe, and are also found in parts of southern Europe, South Asia, North Africa, West Africa and in countries to which Europeans migrated – wherever there was extensive exogamy with northern

Europeans. For example, many Ashkenazi Jewish people have blue eyes, including those now living in Israel. A pre-war study of Ukrainian Jews found that 53.7 per cent had blue eyes.

According to research conducted in Denmark, the countries with the highest blue-eyed percentages are Estonia (99 per cent), followed by Finland and Denmark (89 per cent). In England, Wales and Scotland, between 45 and 50 per cent of people are blue-eyed. In the United States, the proportion is falling rapidly. A study headed by the Chicago epidemiologist Mark Grant found that, while about half of Americans had blue eyes in 1950, this had declined to one in six by 2002. Around 8 per cent of the world's population has blue eyes.

SLAVERY BLUES

The great painters had found their true blue, but for those in the business of dyeing clothes, the search was still on. One candidate was woad, a soil-depleting flowering weed that proliferated in Europe with leaves that produce a blue dye. When Julius Caesar invaded Britain in 55 BC, he wrote that he was confronted by blue, woad-smeared Picts (as the Romans called the Scots). It was a practice also used by the Germanic 'barbarian' tribes, many of whom were blue-eyed, which was considered unfortunate by the Romans. The idea behind painting their bodies with blue woad was that blue skin would scare the invaders. It also had religious undertones, and its antiseptic properties might have helped them recover from wounds.

Later, the Roman colonists who invaded Britain had a run-in with Boudicca, the leader of the Iceni. They flogged her, raped her daughters, seized her land and sold her family into slavery, after she had the temerity to insist on her inheritance rights, prompting her to lead her 100,000 fighters in sacking and burning London, Colchester and St Albans, killing at least 70,000 Romans along the way. Subsequent images of Boudicca have her either painted or tattooed in woad, or wearing a woad-dyed cloak, while riding her chariot.

For several centuries, woad was the European dye of choice and could variously produce dark blue and light blue products, but only after a complicated process that involved removing all oxygen from the vats by fermenting the weed. The item of clothing being dyed would emerge from the vat looking yellowish, but would turn blue when aired, because the chemical reacted with oxygen. It was therefore considered a magical process.

People in Mesopotamia, parts of Asia, Ghana and regions of Africa and the Americas had been dyeing their clothes with

Right: Boudicca in her woad blue cloak.

WHY 'BLUE-SKY' THINKING?
The idea behind this managerial jargon is that, like the blue sky, creative thinking is open-ended in its ambition and refreshingly uninhibited, although using clichés like 'blue-sky' thinking' might suggest otherwise.

indigo for thousands of years. For example, the Tuareg people in West and North Africa have dyed their headscarves with indigo for many centuries, believing this version of blue protected them from evil. They did not object when, inevitably, some of this protective blue rubbed off on their skins, which led to them being known as the 'Blue People'.

Like woad, indigo comes from a type of plant. The woad plant is a member of the cabbage family, while the indigo plant is a member of the bean family. Indigo was probably first cultivated in the Indus Valley, in north-west India, at least 5,000 years ago. The British Museum has a 2,700-year-old tablet containing Babylonian indigo dye recipes that were also used by the Ancient Egyptians. One account, from the thirteenth century BC, describes the lot of the dyer as 'worse than any woman's' and goes on to say that he never breathes pure air, and that if he fails to produce his daily quota 'he is beaten like a lotus in the pond'.

Indigo was preferred to woad for various reasons: the process was cheaper, the plant produced far more dye and the quality of blue was better. Woad was fine for wool but not so good for less absorbent cotton, although English woad dyers were having none of it. They managed to get indigo banned until 1660, on the grounds that it was poisonous, which was untrue. However, the law was largely ignored, particularly by British manufacturers doing business in India, who either used a mix of woad and indigo, for wool, or pure indigo, known as Indian Blue, for cotton.

A Tuareg man wearing his indigo-dyed headscarf (left). The process of dyeing, such as that carried out at dye pits in northern Nigeria, where craftsmen adhere to centuries-old methods of dyeing textiles using indigo (right), can produce the most brilliant blue.

Indigo dye was not popular in India itself, partly because of a belief, held particularly strongly by the upper-class Brahmins, that cloth should be in its natural state and not dyed. It didn't help, either, that indigo blue was the colour of the 'Untouchable' (Sudra) caste and was seen as impure. The result was that if a Brahmin man had anything to do with indigo – even accidentally touching an indigo plant – he lost status.

The caste system placed Indian women at the bottom of the hierarchy, so that even upper-caste women were not banned from contact with indigo. There was a paradox here because blue was perceived more widely in India as a colour with the power to fend off evil – the idea being that it took something vile to keep the 'evil eye' at bay. So it was common for mothers to give bangles of indigo-dyed cotton with blue beads to babies to keep them safe.

Due to the Hindu upper-caste admonition against indigo and blue in general, most of the dyeing in India took place in isolated areas and was carried out by Muslims. The traditional process involved fermenting the blue leaves in urine-filled vats, which would turn a greenish-yellow colour. The cloth was then immersed and, as with woad, it would come out of the vat a pale yellow colour, before turning blue with exposure to oxygen in the air.

The mass production of indigo spread to the French West Indies, early in the seventeenth century, with its ideal climate and abundance of slave labour. There was also local knowledge, because some of the slaves were Yoruba people, who had used indigo to dye their textiles in Nigeria. By the mid-seventeenth century, Caribbean indigo had edged out Indian Blue in the world market. When the English went to war with the French a century later, they lost this new source of dye for their uniforms.

WHY ARE THE MOST RELIABLE STOCKS AND COMPANIES CALLED 'BLUE-CHIP'?

In 1923, Oliver Gingold, a Dow Jones reporter, who dabbled in poker, was eyeing a rolling stock ticker and spotted several stocks trading at more than $200, prompting him to remark that he would go back to his office to 'write about these blue-chips stocks'. Poker players bet in blue, white and red chips, with the blues having twenty-five times the value of the whites, and five times the value of the reds. Thus, the term 'blue chip' came to signify high quality and aspiration.

Enter sixteen-year-old Eliza Lucas, an English girl whose family had settled in South Carolina a year earlier. Her father, George, went off to fight the Spaniards in 1739. Eliza was put in charge of their 600-acre estate, which included sixty slaves. Their rice crop wasn't paying the bills, so her father – by now posted in Antigua, in the Caribbean – started sending her seeds. Alfalfa and ginger crops both failed, but the next envelope to arrive contained indigo seeds.

Eliza's first indigo crop was blighted by frost, but George then employed a young grower, Nicholas Cromwell, to help Eliza. However, Cromwell was worried that her success would eclipse his own family's plantation, so he sabotaged her vats with lime. Eliza was a fighter, though, and she spotted Cromwell's deceit, so she fired him, only to find that the next indigo crop was being devoured by caterpillars. Finally, Eliza got it right, and her fourth crop flourished in 1744, the same year that George died as a prisoner-of-war of the French.

Most indigo growers would have striven to guard their knowledge, but not the far-sighted Eliza. She married a

Below: A depiction of an indigo plantation in South Carolina in Eliza Lucas's day.

neighbouring planter, Charles Pinckney, and donated seeds to other farmers in the area while also offering advice, with the idea of establishing a South Carolina indigo industry, big enough to serve the needs of the British military. By 1755 they were exporting almost 500 tons of indigo dye per year – with the plantation slaves doing all the hard work.

The American indigo industry flourished for forty years or so, but when the British lost their American colony, the South Carolina farmers lost their market. Britain then revived India's indigo industry, much to the dismay of the higher castes, and switched to the brutal exploitation of Indian labour. This prompted riots in 1870 and Mahatma Gandhi's first act of civil disobedience in India in 1917, in support of the northern Bihar indigo peasant workers.

Eliza, who died of cancer at the age of seventy in 1793, relied on seeds sent from Antigua but she might have used an indigenous indigo plant species. A more resilient, weather-resistant and insect-resistant indigo plant had been used by Native Americans for centuries as part of a thriving North American indigo industry, which had supplied the Maya of the Yucatan peninsula and the Aztecs of Mexico, who used it both as a medicine and a dye. As part of their human sacrifice ceremonies, the Aztecs would paint their victims with indigo blue before ripping their hearts out.

INDIGO BLUE JEANS

Carolinian indigo had one lasting cultural contribution: blue jeans. The story starts in the mid-nineteenth century, with a young German Jewish businessman called Levi Strauss, who had migrated to New York at the age of eighteen. He was in the wholesale business and was rather peripatetic, moving from St Louis, Missouri, then to Louisville, Kentucky and finally to San Francisco, where he sold the goods his brothers sent from New York, including cotton cloth made in New Hampshire called *de Nimes*, named after the town of Nimes in the south of France. Thus '*de Nimes*' evolved into 'denim'.

Above: An early advert for Levi's jeans, which focused on the cloth's practicle uses.

His best customer was a Latvian Jewish immigrant called Jacob Youphes, who changed his name to Davis after arriving in New York aged twenty-three. Like Strauss, Davis lived an itinerant life for a while – as a gold prospector and a salesman of tobacco and pork – before returning to his former profession as a tailor and settling in Reno, Nevada, where he made tents, horse blankets and wagon covers from the denim cloth he bought from Levi Strauss.

Shortly before Christmas in 1870 one of Davis's customers asked him to make a pair of working trousers for her woodcutter husband. Using duck cloth (a type of linen canvas), he made the trousers and strengthened the seams and pockets with copper rivets. The woodcutter was delighted and soon all of his friends and fellow labourers wanted a pair. Davis got to work, switching from duck cloth to denim, and soon demand outstripped supply, so he approached his supplier with a business proposition and they signed a partnership contract. The wholesaler put up the money and supplied the denim; the tailor moved to San Francisco and oversaw production.

Strauss and Davis took out a patent, at first calling their product 'waist overalls', but later switched to the catchier jeans, a word derived from the trousers worn by sailors in Genoa. As indigo was the cheapest available dye, their jeans were duly coloured blue. Jacobs added a label on the back pocket, after which they became known as Levi's, or, generically, as 'blue jeans'.

At first they were used solely as work clothes. For example, an 1899 Levi Strauss and Co. advertisement is headed 'Patent Riveted Clothing' and carries a picture of a farmer tilling the field wearing blue jeans and a blue denim shirt (by then they were also producing shirts and overalls). The advertisement notes they are 'The Best in Use for Farmers, Mechanics and Miners'.

During the Second World War, some of the materials became scarce, including the cotton used for the inner seams and pockets, and the copper for the rivets. This increased demand, and after the war the jeans became a much-desired fashion item – a symbol of 1950s rock 'n' roll rebellion, an icon of, alternatively, hippie culture and country music culture, of high fashion and even royalty. Hollywood helped make them an international staple.

Indigo has long since been replaced by synthetic dyes and today black jeans are an alternative, among many other colours but, by a long way, blue jeans remain the most popular choice – a tribute, in a sense, to indigo's role in nineteenth-century American life.

Strauss died in 1902, six years before Davis, with a fortune of $6 million ($170 million in today's money). Today their company employs 16,000 people worldwide.

Opposite: Levi's jeans were originally used solely as work clothes by miners and labourers.

WHY ARE MANUAL WAGE EARNERS CALLED 'BLUE-COLLAR' WORKERS?

It's an indigo thing again. The term was coined in the late nineteenth century when most manual workers wore shirts with blue, indigo-dyed collars, which could hold more dirt than white ones, without being noticed.

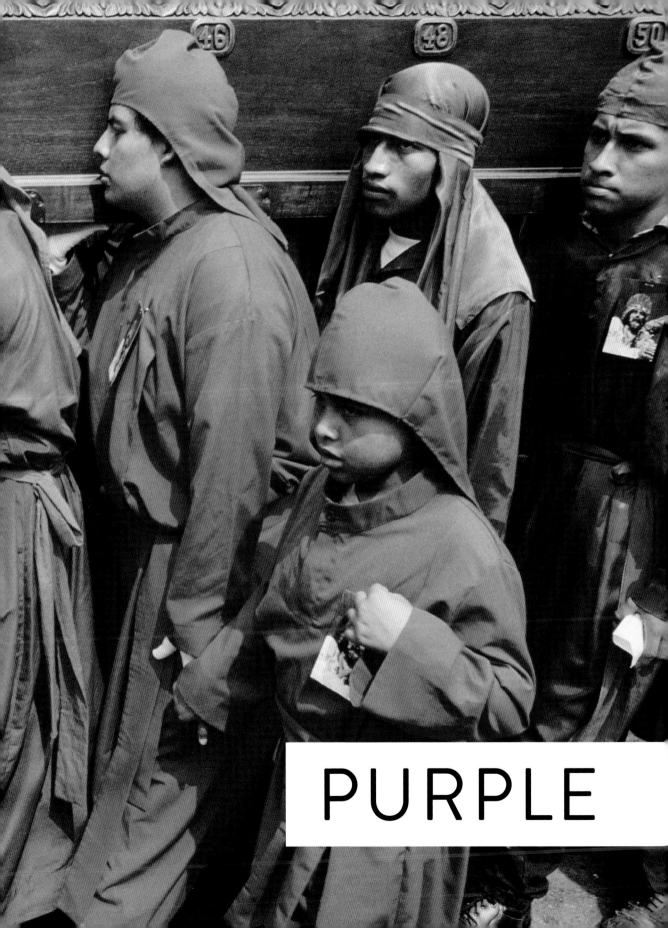

PURPLE

PURPLE WAS ONCE THE COLOUR FOR ROYALTY – often a colour no one else was allowed to wear, sometimes on pain of death. This was because purple was extremely expensive to produce from natural sources, and so it became associated with the very wealthy. It stayed that way in Europe from Roman times until the invention of synthetic purple dye in 1856. As a result, purple reached the heights of fashion in the late nineteenth century, becoming affordable to the middle classes for the first time.

In the 1960s purple had another period of popularity, this time as the colour of the counter-culture, often associated with defiance, psychedelia and androgyny. In the twenty-first century, it has been popular again as an alternative feminine colour. It has also become associated with gay men – in the words of the gay film director and artist Derek Jarman: 'The blue of men and the red of women combine to make queer purple.' Along the way, deep purple became an option as a funereal colour (see previous page), because it was said to symbolize penitence and mourning, a custom continued in contemporary Thailand, where widows frequently wear purple.

In Japan and parts of Latin America it is also associated with death. This tradition was fostered in Britain by Queen Victoria upon the death of her husband, Prince Albert, and continued until the 1950s. For instance, when the current Queen's father, King George VI, died in 1952, mauve underwear was displayed in West End shop windows.

Purple picked up more specific meanings in other parts of the world. In Spain, if one over-indulged in food and wine, one was said 'to purple'. In English, as the Dilly Dally lyric put it, 'I got that purple rage'. Anger is red, but rage is purple. Both relate to the colour of people's faces when they really lose their temper. For the Japanese, Russians and Poles, purple is also associated with envy and jealousy.

Perhaps more than any other colour today, purple lends itself to the spiritual. If one searches the internet for 'meanings of purple' one comes across claims like: 'purple combines the calm stability of blue and the fierce energy of red'. One reads that it represents

peace, devotion, mystery and magic; that it uplifts spirits, calms nerves, enhances the sacred, increases nurturing tendencies and sensitivity, encourages imagination and creativity, and that it is associated with the higher self and the 'Third Eye' and helps to align oneself with the whole of the universe.

So what is purple? In the song 'I Can Sing a Rainbow', it is one of the colours of the spectrum. In Newton's Roy G Biv version, this same colour is called violet, the last one on the list, and the only one to be named after a flower. Purple synthetic dye was, originally, called mauve. Colour specialists insist these are really different shades – purple is more saturated and reddish; violet is less saturated and bluish; mauve is a paler shade of purple. In the paintbox they are all mixes of blues and reds, some with a bit of white thrown in, and in everyday speech the words are often used interchangeably.

Previous page: The Emperor Justinian swathed in a mantle of purple, a shade so expensive to produce in his time, the sixth century AD, that often only royalty were permitted to wear it.

DIFFERENT WORDS FOR PURPLE?

Purple has taken ages to acquire its current definition. This is largely because Tyrian purple – an ancient term named after Tyre in Phoenicia – could be anything from blood red to purple to bright blue. The production of purple dye was unpredictable, so that different hues resulted. Also, the pigments would fade in different ways. A sample of wool said to be dyed with Tyrian purple, exhibited in the National Museum of Beirut, is now pink.

Now that we have more definition, we need more words. Aside from purple, mauve and violet, purplish shades include lilac, plum, fuchsia, puce, aubergine, wine, lavender, magenta, perse, periwinkle, amaranthine and heliotrope.

ROYAL PURPLE

When Cleopatra's barge sailed into harbour, the first thing people noticed was the purple sail. As William Shakespeare's Enobarbus put it in Act 2 of *Antony and Cleopatra*:

> The barge she sat in, like a burnish'd throne,
> Burned on the water: the poop was beaten gold;
> Purple the sails, and so perfumed that
> The winds were lovesick with them.

Shakespeare sometimes played fast and loose with history, bending it to fit the needs of his art, but on this detail he was correct – Cleopatra's boats really did have purple sails and it is likely they were perfumed because in those days purple was a particularly smelly colour. Contemporary reports suggest that it wasn't only her sails – her palaces had purple sofas and drapes. Cleopatra wasn't the first to use purple. The method for making

Below: Cleopatra on her barge on the River Cydnus, surrounded by her chosen colour and, overleaf, her ship with its purple sails.

Tyrian purple is thought to have been discovered nearly 4,000 years ago. A process is described in Phoenician writing from 1600 BC, which spread to the Persians, Egyptians, Greeks and Jews. According to writers of Exodus 26:1, God instructed that the Tabernacle, which housed the Arc of the Covenant, should be made with 'ten curtains of fine twined linen and blue and purple and scarlet yarns'. The last book of the Christian Bible, Revelation (19:11-12), talks about the Apocalypse leading to the fall of Babylon and predicts the merchants will weep because no one will buy their products any more, including 'fine linen, purple silk and scarlet cloth'.

But it was the Romans who did most to enhance the status of Tyrian purple. They conquered Greece in 146 BC, making it a province of their Empire, after which they began to absorb Greek ideas, myths, gods, fashions, art and colours. Julius Caesar visited Egypt in 48 BC, and was seduced by their Greek-speaking queen Cleopatra. He was so impressed with her sumptuous, purple accessorized surroundings that, when he returned home, he decreed that purple would henceforth be an exclusively royal colour – one that only consuls were permitted to wear. Before that, Roman togas worn by wealthier citizens had a purple band, victorious soldiers could wear purple and gold, and generals wore purple cloaks.

After Julius Caesar and in the time of the Empire, the rules regarding purple varied according to who was in power. Some emperors were more protective – none more so than Nero, who banned purple for anyone but himself. The rest of his household were ordered to dress in red. The penalty for disobeying was execution. Some of Nero's successors, however, were less restrictive. In the second and third centuries AD, high-ranking generals were once again permitted to wear purple and they were even more lenient with noblewomen. The most liberal of the emperors was Diocletian, who ruled from AD 284 to 305. He allowed all of his citizens to wear purple but with one caveat: they paid prohibitive taxes for the honour.

For the vast majority of citizens this wasn't an option because purple was alarmingly expensive – it was worth between ten and twenty times its weight in gold. Even if one had the money, one might not have had the nose because Tyrian purple was distinctly fishy in odour.

To produce one gram of Tyrian purple it was necessary to process 12,000 murex sea snails. Even though the snails were farmed, the process was highly labour intensive, so the dye was prohibitively expensive. The process involved crushing the snails

to expose the gland that produces the precious fluid, which was extracted and then mixed with wood ash and urine and fermented for ten days. The dye is colourless in its natural state but turns purple with exposure to air. However, it also fades very quickly in sunlight, so the processing was required to 'fix' the colour. White cloth would be dipped in and would emerge one or another shade of purple, and sometimes pink or blue, depending on the exact species of sea snail.

The murex sea snail, the creature responsible for the base of Tyrian purple.

Pliny the Elder, the patrician historian, noted in his *Natural History* that the Tyrian colour could range between red, purple and blue-black, but was best when it was 'the colour of clotted blood'. Whichever version came out of the pot, it looked lovely and didn't fade, but it stank. The vats in Tyre were placed beyond the city walls because of their disgusting reek of rotting shellfish and urine. The dyed clothes didn't smell pleasant either – Pliny described them as smelling 'offensive'.

Tyrian purple found its way to China where, by about AD 300, it had been added to the list of acceptable colours, and was said to represent the harmony of the universe. Production also transferred to Constantinople when the Roman Empire split, and its emperors maintained the tradition of royal purple. European royalty adopted the custom, again restricting the colour to their own ranks. For example, Charlemagne was crowned, in AD 800, wearing a mantle dyed in Tyrian purple, and he was buried in a shroud of the same colour.

Right: A portion of the shroud of Charlemagne, which employed imperial Tyrian purple and gold thread to represent the power and majesty of the founder of the Carolingian Empire.

WHY ARE ALTARS DRAPED IN PURPLE DURING LENT?

This comes from Gospel references to Jesus being mockingly cloaked in a purple robe before and after being scourged. As John's Gospel puts it: 'And the soldiers twisted together a crown of thorns and put it on His head, and put a purple robe on Him; and they began to come up to Him and say, "Hail, King of the Jews!" and to give Him slaps in the face.'

By the time Constantinople fell to the Muslims (1453), the process method had long been lost and was only rediscovered in the mid-seventeenth century. In the interim, red (from cochineal dye) had become the alternative royal colour, with purple being created by mixing indigo with red dye, but wasn't of the same high quality as the Tyrian purple of old. In other parts of the world better sources had been found. For instance, the Japanese used dye extracted from *murasaki* root for dyeing their purple kimonos, from around AD 800.

Purple continued to be restricted to royalty in Europe. During the Elizabethan era purple could only be worn by the queen and her relations, although dukes, earls and marquises were allowed it in the lining of their cloaks. Once the sumptuary laws were abandoned throughout Europe in the seventeenth century, it became a colour more widely used by other notables, including bishops and university professors and doctoral graduates.

THE MAUVE DECADE

In 1856, William Henry Perkin, an eighteen-year-old chemistry student at the Royal College of Chemistry, was asked to conduct an experiment. London had started installing coal-gas powered street lamps, which meant that coal tar was in plentiful supply as a by-product of the gas manufacturing process. Perkin's task was to discover whether the hydrocarbons among the fractions might be used as a malaria cure. The only available medication was quinine, made from the bark of the cinchona tree, so the aim was to discover a cheaper synthetic form of quinine, as the British Empire included many colonies in malaria-ridden locations.

Perkin used a small room on the third floor of his parents' East London flat. After several attempts, he failed to isolate anything that looked like it might work. All he had produced was unpromising sludge. Then, in his final attempt, which involved mixing coal aniline with chromic acid, he noticed something intriguing when cleaning the aniline out of his flasks. He dipped a piece of cloth in the sludge and it came out purple. 'The solution resulted in a strangely beautiful colour,' he recalled many years later. A few days on, it still held its colour without fading, and Perkin had his eureka moment. With a nod to history, he first called it 'Tyrian purple', but after a bit more thought he chose 'mauveine' combining 'mauve' with 'aniline'. In 1857 he patented his synthetic purple dye.

Within a year Perkin's mauveine was being mass-produced, the first ever cheap, effective synthetic dye. Its popularity was immense and it spread all over the world. In 1859 *Punch* magazine referred to 'Mauve Measles' (pronounced 'morve' at the time, incidentally). The following year Prince Albert died, and Queen Victoria appeared in a mauve mourning dress, after which her subjects felt they should follow suit and it became the colour of funereal attire.

By the late Victorian era, purple had reached its zenith, with high society women showing their pedigree in purple, and none more so than the imperious, six-foot tall Chicago-born Mary

Perkin's original mauve dye. The bottle reads: Original mauveine prepared by Sir William Perkin in 1856.

Victoria Leiter, who became Lady Curzon, Vicereine of India (said to be part of the inspiration behind the *Downton Abbey* character Lady Grantham). She was utterly obsessed with 'morve' – for dresses, coats, tablecloths at her dinners, flowers in her house; she even insisted that the sweets in her house were wrapped in purple.

Within a few decades, there were around 2,000 synthetic dyes on the market. Coal was used for several, including magenta, alizarin red and synthetic indigo. Perkin's success encouraged chemical companies to see what else they could find from aniline in coal tar, prompting the discovery of saccharine, fertilizers, perfumes, medicines, explosives and food preservatives, as well as numerous other synthetic dyes. In 1874, aged thirty-six, Perkin retired a wealthy man.

THE PURPLE DECADE

Each season, a fresh range of colours dominates fashion in retail. Most of us don't have a clue where they come from, but all the stores seem to be on the same page, more or less, and this is no coincidence. In fact, the colours are decided upon a good two years beforehand. So how does this happen?

In 1915 a group of American textile manufacturers wanted to get their colours right for their clothing ranges at a time when the first department stores were opening. So they banded together to establish The Color Association of the United States (CAUS), which took on the task of making recommendations on the colours to define each season.

After more than a century, CAUS is still going strong – indeed, it has inspired similar organizations in other countries – and has a profound influence on the seasonal colours chosen by the fashion industry, from catwalk designs to off-the-peg store garments and also the cosmetics industry. How they do this might sound a bit ephemeral to the outsider. 'We really try to capture a feeling or zeitgeist of what's going on in society,' said the CAUS director of

Opposite: A selection of CAUS colour cards for evening shades from 1922, representing colours chosen for the fall season.

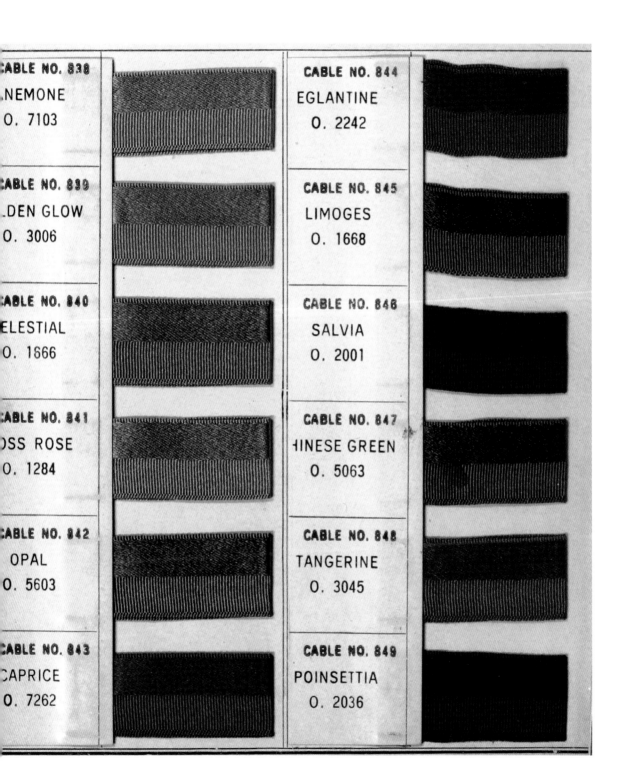

CABLE NO. 838
NEMONE
O. 7103

CABLE NO. 844
EGLANTINE
O. 2242

CABLE NO. 839
DEN GLOW
O. 3006

CABLE NO. 845
LIMOGES
O. 1668

CABLE NO. 840
ELESTIAL
O. 1666

CABLE NO. 846
SALVIA
O. 2001

CABLE NO. 841
OSS ROSE
O. 1284

CABLE NO. 847
HINESE GREEN
O. 5063

CABLE NO. 842
OPAL
O. 5603

CABLE NO. 848
TANGERINE
O. 3045

CABLE NO. 843
CAPRICE
O. 7262

CABLE NO. 849
POINSETTIA
O. 2036

147

colour trends, Roseanna Roberts, in *Time* magazine. She added 'Anything from architecture and films to events, like the Olympics or elections; even a person who has been touted as someone who will be making waves … We've had committee members come in with a stone they found on a street, a scrap of fabric, a flower, a spice, anything that really has colour.'

CAUS looks at least two years ahead and uses trends in everyday life that it thinks might have resonance. It sends committee members (buyers, manufacturers and designers) to compile research on the colours that are trending. They work with dyers to come up with colour cards, which are distributed to their members at least eighteen months before the relevant season. In some years, several colours dominate, only to be replaced the next season. At other times, one colour will stand out and will have a more lasting impact because it seems to capture the spirit of the age in a way that is definitive. Which brings us back to purple.

It is hard to pinpoint a precise moment when this colour thrust itself into the cultural foreground, but perhaps the Summer of Love, the Haight-Ashbury neighbourhood and San Francisco, 1967, would fit. It was then that the words 'hippie' and 'flower

Below: Purple's peak was arguably the Summer of Love in 1967, when it captured the zeitgeist and was the colour of the hippie movement.

power' entered the lexicon – capturing the idea of tuning in, turning on and dropping out, as author Tim Leary put it; of taking LSD and other psychedelic drugs, of listening to acid rock and other alternative music at festivals, of opposing the Vietnam War and eschewing conventional fashion, values and morality. It was a spirit captured by Scott McKenzie's 1967 song 'San Francisco', which talks of 'gentle people with flowers in their hair'. Once the media took up the story, the message of the Summer of Love spread very quickly.

What anyone with their eyes on colour trends would have noticed was the abundance of purple in all this – purplish hair flowers, purple peace signs, love signs and other motifs, purple-framed posters, purple tie-dye granny vest shirts, blouses and tops and so on, and these were soon worn by young people in Paris, London, Berlin, Tokyo, Stockholm and all over the globe. Jimi Hendrix absorbed these new meanings with his trippy song 'Purple Haze', which ends with the note that this haze is confusing his mind.

Naturally, the fashion industry embraced the trend with great vigour and by the end of the decade were mass-producing purple clothes for both sexes. So it was, that this one colour helped give definition to a few precious years of history. Writing in his white suit and fedora, with bitter distaste for the values of the time, Tom Wolfe dubbed it 'the purple decade' and published a book of his own writing under that title, but really the purple trend exploded to capture a few years in the late 1960s and early 1970s, and then quickly receded.

Heroin addiction and drug overdoses, the deaths of Janis Joplin, Jimi Hendrix and Jim Morrison, the killing of a black concert-goer by Hell's Angels at the Rolling Stones Altamont concert, the Manson family murders and the rise of ultra-left terrorism in the United States, Germany and Italy, all contributed to the sense that the hippie era was over and soon purple became passé, although some of its influence lingered.

For example, in 1968 an English 'progressive rock' group jumped on the bandwagon and called themselves Deep Purple, but quickly succumbed to the influence of Led Zeppelin and morphed into a heavy metal band – more in tune with the zeitgeist of the strutting, posing, coiffured seventies. Still, the musical innings of the colour had one last magnificent moment: the purple-clad Prince, who might be said to be Hendrix's successor as a lead guitar maestro, came out with his *Purple Rain* (single, album and film) fifteen years after Jimi's death, offering a darker, eighties version of the purple mood.

THE PURPLE RAIN
PROTEST

Five years after Prince's hit song, South Africa's apartheid police had what they thought was an inspired purple rain idea (one first applied by the British in quelling protests in Northern Ireland). They would put a long-lasting purple dye in the water for their water cannon and mount it on an armoured car with the idea that, when faced with demonstrators, they would spray them, and those with purple clothes and faces could then be detained without trial.

They got their big chance on 2 September 1989, when protesters in Cape Town marched against the forthcoming whites-only elections for South Africa's segregated parliament. The police banned the march, so the protesters staged a sit-in and faced baton charges, tear gas and beatings with *sjamboks* (police whips).

Then, the police got to work with their water cannon, which was turned on the demonstrators. Some fled; others knelt down and took the full blast. Then, an intrepid young student, a doctor's son, climbed on top of a police vehicle and turned the nozzle in the direction of the regional headquarters of the ruling National Party, covering it in the same purple dye, and soon the demonstrators were laughing in the purple rain.

The police detained hundreds of purple-clad people including a group holding a banner bearing the well-known South African

WHY IS PROSE SOMETIMES PURPLE?

From its royal origins came the connection between purple and writing that was too gushing and opulent. It goes back to Horace who wrote in *The Art of Poetry*: 'Weighty openings and grand declarations often have one or two purple patches tacked on, that gleam far and wide, when Diana's grove and her altar, the winding stream hastening through lovely fields, or the river Rhine, or the rainbow's being described. There's no place for them here.' Today it refers to any writing that is flowery, or ornate, or over-the-top. It tries too hard – too many tired adjectives, adverbs, similes and metaphors.

150

slogan, 'The People Shall Govern', drawn from the ANC's 1955 'Freedom Charter'. Later that day, graffiti artists got to work on the subject of what became known as 'The Purple Rain protest', going from one railway station to the next spraying: 'Free our leaders, unban the ANC and Forward to purple people's power.' The slogan 'The Purple Shall Govern' then appeared very prominently on a wall of the Old Townhouse in the city's Greenmarket Square. Six months later the ANC and other organizations were unbanned, and Nelson Mandela was released from prison.

But the apartheid police's purple plan had a longer-lasting effect: law enforcement in several other countries took note. In 2008 Indian police in the city of Srinagar used purple dye to spray government employees demonstrating for higher pay, with the idea of tagging them for subsequent arrest. However, shopkeepers, rickshaw drivers and journalists were also hit by the dye sprayed from the cannons.

In Kampala, Uganda the police used a purple-dye water cannon to spray opposition party leaders demonstrating against President Yoweri Museveni's autocratic government in 2011.

The Indonesian and South Korean police used pink dye for this purpose, while the Israeli police have used purple and blue dyes to spray both Palestinian and Israeli demonstrators in the West Bank, Gaza and Israel.

Blue is also the colour chosen by the Bangladeshi police when curbing demonstrations on the streets of Dhaka. In 2006 Hungarian police used green dye to spray demonstrators in Budapest and two years later the South Korean police used orange dye on demonstrators protesting against the visit of US President George W. Bush to Seoul.

Below: Indian police fire coloured water at protesting government employees – just one example of the use of purple dye by law enforcement around the world.

PINK

PINK IS A NEW COLOUR – relatively speaking. There is no natural pink paint pigment and through most of history the range of shades we now call pink didn't have a name of their own – they were simply lighter reds, just like lighter blues are shades of blue.

In the seventeenth and eighteenth centuries, the popularity of pink in painting, ceramics and clothing was growing, particularly in France, where it was called *rose* or *roze* or *rose Pompadour,* because it was adored by the king's mistress. In most European languages the colour pink comes from the rose – *rosa* in Spanish, German, Italian, Norwegian and Swedish, *roze* in Dutch, *roz* in Romanian, *rosa* in Portuguese, *różowy* in Polish, *růžový* in Czech and *ružičasta* in Croatian). The use of rose or pink has a far older vintage in several other parts of the world – in ceramics in China and Japan and in fabrics in India. However, its current cultural connotations took a while to arrive.

In English, the word 'pink' originally meant a version of yellow lightened with chalk – unless you were into foxhunting in which case it would suggest a deep red ('donning one's pinks'). It was also a term used to describe a frilled edge, which is why scissors that cut zigzags are called 'pinking shears' – and it was via this path that today's pink emerged. The pale red dianthus or carnation flowers were known as 'pinks' because of the notches in their petals, which looked like they'd been trimmed with pinking shears, and so through this circuitous route, in the late seventeenth century, the word 'pink' became associated with pale red and became its own colour.

Today, pink is slanted in the feminine direction – for little girls' toys, fairy dresses and shoes and women's cars and phones; it is also the ribbon colour of the breast cancer campaign; it was the colour of downward-facing triangles used by the Nazis to brand gay men – which is why it has since been reclaimed to become one of the symbols of gay pride. Meanwhile, in Japan, 'pink films'

Right: In the late 1970s the upside-down pink triangle was adopted as a symbol for gay rights protest, having been reclaimed from the pink Nazi concentration camp badge for gay male prisoners. It has also been used on memorials for gay victims of the Nazis.

were those featuring 'soft porn'. Sometimes the meaning of pink depends on its context. Bright magenta pink and black together has raunchier connotations than pale pink with white spots. But none of this is any way innate to the colour. Perhaps more than with any other colour, the meanings of pink have changed over a short period of time.

WHAT IS PINK MONEY?

Also known as the Dorothy Dollar, the Pink Dollar and the Pink Pound, it refers to the gay community's fiscal pulling power in the market. Many businesses cater specifically for gay clientele, including taxicabs, airlines, nightclubs, restaurants, wedding services, publications, music, cosmetic companies and even builders and plumbers, with advertising homing in on gay people. There have been a range of estimates of the fiscal pulling power of gay men and lesbians, with one American survey putting it at $2 trillion in 2012.

PINK IS FOR BOYS

A team of evolutionary psychologists and neuroscientists from the University of Newcastle-upon-Tyne embarked on a rather odd project in 2007. They started with the notion that women had evolved through natural selection to prefer pink and men, blue. They tested this, by flashing up pairs of colours to 208 British students, with a subgroup of thirty-seven Chinese students, asking these volunteers to select the colour they liked best by clicking a computer mouse. Perhaps a bit to their surprise, the most favoured colour for the women, as well as the men, was blue, confirming the consistent results of previous studies in other parts of the world, which show that blue is, by a long way, the favourite colour of both sexes. However, much to their relief, the women liked pink a bit more than the men.

The researchers believed that a preference for pink evolved biologically, so the team devised retrospective solutions. On the origins of blue-preference, team leader Dr Anya Hurlbert said: 'Going back to our savannah days we would have a natural preference for a blue sky because it signalled good weather. Clear blue also signals a good water source.' But it was her explanation for female pink preference that drew the headlines: 'The explanation might date back to humans' hunter-gatherer days, when women were the primary gatherers and would have benefited from an ability to home in on ripe, red fruits,' she said. She did not explain how it was that liking ripe red fruit prompted a preference for pink or how it might have given those with the right genes any kind of selective advance, let alone whether random genetic mutations for red-preference traits was even a theoretical possibility.

Despite these caveats, their conclusions were energetically embraced by numerous media outlets all over the world. *The Times* headed theirs with, 'At last, science discovers why blue is for boys but girls really do prefer pink', and their introduction to the piece left no doubt: 'Now it emerges that parents who dress their boys in blue and girls in pink may not just be following tradition but some deep-seated evolutionary instinct.' *Time* magazine suggested that 'women may be biologically programmed to prefer the colour pink'.

Above: We can see from these paintings (*The Pink Boy*, Thomas Gainsborough, 1782, and *Portrait of a Pink Boy in a Sailor Suit*, Jacques-Emile Blanche, early twentieth century) that dressing boys in pink had been widely accepted long before the reversal in trends in the twentieth century.

Ben Goldacre, however, in his 'Bad Science' column in the *Guardian*, noted that the test was devised to measure preference rather than ability to discern shades of red, which might have conferred a berry-picking edge. The more decisive verdict came from publication archives, which he and other sceptics dug up. These showed that the pink-for-girls tradition was a very recent phenomenon.

For example, back in 1897, *The New York Times* ran an article on 'Baby's First Wardrobe' in which they advised: 'The pink is usually considered the colour for a boy and the blue for a girl, but mothers use their own taste in such matters.'

Seventeen years later the advice in the *American Sunday Sentinel* was more emphatic, instructing mothers to 'use pink for a boy and blue for a girl, if you are a follower of convention'. It wasn't only in America. In 1918 the *British Ladies' Home Journal* noted: 'The generally accepted rule is pink for the boy and blue for the girl. The reason is that pink being a more decided and stronger colour is more suitable for the boy, while blue, which is more delicate and dainty, is prettier for the girl.'

One reason why pink was seen as masculine at this time was because of its association with blood red – a bright and light, little boys' version of this manly colour. In other countries, including India, the bolder pinks had strong masculine connotations for men as well as boys.

In 1927 there was a colour skirmish among American companies behind children's clothes. Manufacturers in New York and Los Angeles promoted pink as a boys' colour, while those in Chicago, Philadelphia and New Orleans promoted it as a girls' colour. For the most part pink and pale blue were used interchangeably for babies and children. Sometimes blonde, blue-eyed children were dressed in blue, and brown-haired children in pink, and in the 1950s pink clothes for boys were still being manufactured widely in the United States, particularly for the spring season because the colour was seen as vibrant, energetic and youthful.

In 1946, Sugar Ray Robinson, rated by many as the finest boxer of all time, won the first of his six world titles and celebrated by buying the first of many Cadillacs. His colour of choice was pink. Sugar Ray was a violent man who beat up his women as well as men. He once killed a man in the ring and knocked out 108 of his professional opponents but no one blinked at his flamboyant choice of bright pink.

Below: Boxer Sugar Ray Robinson leaning on his 1950 pink Cadillac convertible in front of his two businesses.

Right: Marketing for girls' clothing in the 1950s was now weighted heavily towards pink.

However, when he continued using pink Cadillacs and as his career lingered into the 1960s, sniggers were heard. By then, mainly through advertising campaigns, pink had been redefined as a feminine and even effeminate colour.

Drab-looking clothes, cars and furnishings dominated during the Second World War, but once it was over, advertisers wanted to take advantage of post-war optimism, by promoting brighter colours, and so it was that the 1950s became the 'pink decade' in the US. This time, pink was steered exclusively in the direction of girls and women – perhaps just because it had been tending that way since the 1930s.

WHY ARE FLAMINGOS PINK?

It was once thought that they evolved this way because pink gave them some selective advantage. In fact, it has everything to do with their diet. They eat brine shrimps and crustaceans that are rich in carotenoid – a reddish pigment.

SHOCKING PINK

In 1937, the Surrealist designer Elsa Schiaparelli launched a perfume in a bottle shaped like a woman's body – supposedly modelled on the actress Mae West. It appeared in a box with a new shade that she called 'Shocking Pink' – she got the idea from a pink diamond worn by her socialite friend Daisy Fellowes, describing it as 'bright, impossible, impudent, becoming, life-giving ... a shocking colour'.

Schiaparelli dubbed her creation 'Shocking' and it was soon known as 'the first sex perfume' – in tribute to its colour, curvy bottle and particular scent. 'Shocking pink' became a women's magazine title and then morphed into a euphemism for the vagina in some circles.

The link between pink and products designed for women, pushing a certain perception of femininity, was established. Avon Cosmetics promoted pink lipstick and nail polish, and film stars began to dress in pink. *Mademoiselle* magazine featured an all-pink work suit on one of its covers and Teena Paige Fashions promoted its pink party dresses. Dodge launched its 1955 pink-and-white 'La Femme' model (complete with lipstick holder and complementary pink umbrella) with the slogan, 'Never a car more distinctively feminine ... first fine car created exclusively for women!'

This soon settled into public consciousness, aided by popular 1950s songs, such as 'Think Pink!' from the Audrey Hepburn musical *Funny Face*, 'Pink Champagne', 'Cherry Pink and Apple Blossom White', 'Pink Cadillac', 'Pink Chiffon', 'A Touch of Pink' and many more. The change happened more gradually in some other countries – blue and pink were still being used for both girls

Advertising the colour pink in the 1950s and 1960s was ubiquitous, with leading brands and manufacturers such as Avon pushing pink-branded products for women. This reached as far as the car industry, with Dodge creating a pink model solely for female use.

WHY ARE SOCIALISTS CALLED 'PINKOS'?
The term started as one of derision, the idea being that they were watered-down reds. It goes back to a story in *Time* magazine in 1925, which mentioned 'parlour-pink' socialists who showed sympathy for the communism of the Soviet Union, but did nothing about it. The contemporary equivalent would be 'champagne socialists'.

A magazine advert from US cosmetics company Elizabeth Arden, titled 'Pink Perfection', promoted pink lipstick and nail varnish to the female market (left); pink adverts from the 1960s continued the association of pink with femininity, telling readers, unequivocally, that 'pink is for girls' (below left and right).

PINK
IS FOR GIRLS

That's why girls like Lustre-Creme is pink. Because it's made just for girls. If you don't believe it, just breathe in Lustre-Creme's pink fragrance. See. It is a little too delicate for anyone but a girl! Now shampoo with pink Lustre-Creme and feel how truly soft your hair can be. So soft, it says "touch me." And he will!

PINK IS FOR GIRLS

That's why girls like Lustre-Creme. It's the only pink shampoo.
Pink says we're rich, so rich your whole head becomes
one great swirl of whipped-cream lather.
Pink says we leave hair soft, and inviting to touch.
And should a certain someone get too close, he'll notice
that we have a delightful "pink" fragrance, too.
Pink, creamy Lustre-Creme. It's the one shampoo
made just for girls. Because pink is just for girls.
You're a girl, aren't you?

and boys, sometimes together in pink-and-blue garments, as late as the 1980s in Belgium and Switzerland.

What all this suggests is that the current female preference for pink has nothing to do with genes, and everything to do with culture. Yet it's hard to shake off the notion that pink is essentially girly. So how does that happen? The answer may relate to the process we all go through from as early as six months old in developing awareness of ourselves as girls or boys. Right from the start, girl babies are smothered in pink and boys in blue. By the time they're aware of their gender, well before their second birthdays, girls associate their femininity with pink and by the time they grow up, this constantly reinforced preference feels natural.

Over the last couple of decades feminists in the United States, Britain, Australia, France, Germany, Scandinavia and several other countries have campaigned against the division of children's toys into pink and blue categories – dolls, tea sets and fairy skirts for girls; building blocks, dinosaurs and balls for boys. One way around the problem would be to tackle the association of pink with femininity – a tough job, given its cultural ubiquity.

THE 'PINK TAX'

It started in France, in 2014, when their women's minister asked rhetorically, *'Le rose est-il une couleur de luxe?'* – 'Is pink a luxury colour?' It has been reported that pink women's razors were selling for more than double the price of men's razors. The term 'pink tax' went viral when it was discovered that all over the world women paid more for the same products and services than men. For example, a UK study showed that women were paying double for dry-cleaning services for collars and cuffs. There have also been reports of women paying more for car repairs, haircuts, underwear and a range of other products and services.

PRISON PINK

Joe Arpaio relishes his reputation as 'America's toughest sheriff', known for favouring chain gangs for prisoners, who sleep in tents – he once happily measured the daytime temperature inside them at 145°F – giving them just two meals a day and making them pay for their food.

His philosophy involves not giving an inch to inmates, and so, when he discovered that prisoners had been 'stealing' their white prison underwear after serving their sentences, he declared this to be an assault on taxpayers, and devised an underpants solution: 'I had an idea – why not pink?' he said to much fanfare.

Below: A prisoner showing his pink underwear.

Arpaio's thinking went along the lines that pink was a feminine colour so the tough male inmates therefore wouldn't like it and wouldn't want to steal their underpants on leaving. A year on he judged the plan a success, and by then had added pink socks and other items to the package, claiming he had saved the county $70,000. 'They don't like pink,' he gloated. 'They complain sometimes.'

In 2012, however, a court ruled that these pink pants had contributed to the death of a paranoid schizophrenic awaiting trial, who was stripped, held down and dressed in pink by prison officers. The confused thirty-six-year-old looked at his pink pants, yelled that he thought he'd been raped and ran away before dying of a heart attack. The appeal court found that forcing awaiting trial inmates to wear pink 'seems without legal justification'.

This, however, was neither the first not the last use of pink for prisoners. It all started in 1978 when Alexander Schauss, a biology professor from Tacoma, Washington, conducted experiments on the impact of a bright, jaunty shade of pink. He found that men exposed to this shade were weaker in strength tests than those exposed to blue and that it had a calming effect.

A year later the first of several experiments on prisoners was conducted, in the naval holding cells in Seattle, organized by officers Gene Baker and Ron Miller. One of the cells was painted Schauss's colour – thereafter known as Baker-Miller Pink. Levels of prisoner violence plummeted. However, several subsequent academic studies had more ambiguous results, with some showing no link between Baker-Miller Pink and male blood pressure rates or physical strength, and the popularity of what was also dubbed 'drunk tank pink' declined. In 2013 the Swiss belatedly got on board, using Baker-Miller Pink for some of their police cells in a bid to calm men who'd been arrested. The results were declared 'inconclusive'.

WHAT ARE PINK-SHEET STOCKS?

A stock that isn't traded on a major stock exchange is said to trade 'over the counter'. These are usually minor, volatile stocks from unlisted companies. They are said to trade on the 'pink sheets' because they were printed on pink paper (until electronic trading arrived).

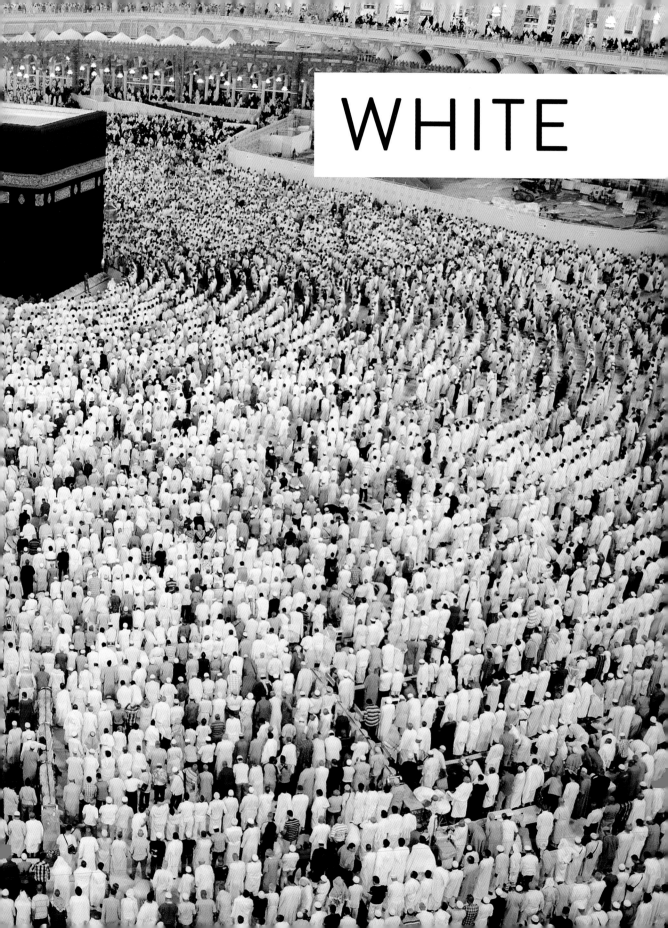

WHITE

WHITE IS THE MIXTURE OF ALL COLOURS when considered in terms of light. However, when we mix all the colours in the paint box we don't get anything resembling white. Instead we get a dirty grey-brown colour. So it is that we tend to think of white, not as the sum of the colours, but as their absence or as the blank template upon which other colours might be displayed.

In much of the world white has become associated with cleanliness, purity and virginity. In nature, its most common associations are with snow and milk. In the Talmudic tradition milk is one of the four sacred substances, while in the Qur'an, it is said that in Jannah – paradise – there will be 'rivers of milk of which the taste never changes' (47:15).

In some pastoral cultures, the colour of milk is also the colour of luck, joy and fertility. The Bedouins of the Negev desert wear white to protect themselves from the Evil Eye and when they pray for protection. Similar associations can be seen in much of Africa. Those among the Hausa people of northern Nigeria view white spirits as being more benevolent and so pour milk on their altars as an offering. They refer to a 'white belly' as representing happiness, and a 'white heart' as representing peace. Muslim men wear two white sheets of cloth during *Ihram*, the state a Muslim must enter to perform the pilgrimage to Mecca (*Hajj*), in order that all pilgrims appear equal.

AS WHITE AS . . .

In fairy tales, white is often the colour of innocence, none more so than in the Brothers Grimm's 1812 Germanic tale *Schneewittchen*, which became the Broadway play *Snow White and the Seven Dwarfs* a century later and was subsequently made into a Disney film. In the original, the humble queen wishes for a daughter with skin white as snow, and when the baby is born, she names her Snow White.

Above: Fair-haired Snow White and dark-haired Rose Red (left); the more traditional depiction of Snow White, with dark hair (right).

Despite the evil plans of her wicked stepmother, she remains good and true. Another, earlier, Brothers Grimm fairy tale, *Schneeweisschen und Rosenrot*, features a fair-haired little girl, also called Snow White, who is shy and loving, and likes to spend her time indoors doing housework and reading – while her lively sister, Rose Red, is robust and outspoken.

DARK WHITE

Yet white is not always passive and sublime. Herman Melville referred to the darkness behind white light in his tale of the sperm whale *Moby Dick*. In chapter two, entitled 'The Whiteness of the Whale' he elaborates on what he sees as the awesome enigma of the colour: 'For all these accumulated associations, with whatever is sweet, and honourable, and sublime, there lurks an elusive something in the innermost idea of this hue, which strikes more panic to the soul than that redness which affrights in blood.'

If we are searching out less wholesome connotations for white, we might add that, from the eighteenth century, the white feather became a symbol of cowardice. During the First World War women would hand them to young men in civilian clothes who had not enlisted. Its origins come from the belief that in cockfighting a rooster with white tail feathers was a poor fighter.

It is also the colour of surrender. The white flag was first used for this purpose in the Han dynasty in China from AD 25, and in Rome in the second century. And it is the colour of a useless and rather troublesome object – the 'white elephant' in the room goes back to sixteenth-century stories of white elephants given as gifts by south-east Asian monarchs, but because they were seen as sacred they could not be put to work.

THE COLOUR OF DEATH

In much of the world, including China, India, Ethiopia, Korea and the Middle East, white is the primary colour of mourning, due to its association with purity, which shows respect to the dead. For example, the European Roma people and Hindus everywhere wear white at funerals and there is an old Indian tradition that widows should wear only white for the rest of their lives.

This deathly white tradition was very much part of the ancient world. In Rome the priestesses of Vesta, the virgin goddess of the hearth, wore white linen robes as a symbol of purity (see image at the start of this chapter), as did the Egyptian priests of Isis, and the mummification process involved bodies being bound in white bandages. Mourning clothes in the European Middle Ages were white – particularly for widows – and this tradition continued among the French royalty until the sixteenth century, while long after that, European children continued to wear white for mourning. Even today, with black as the prime colour of mourning in the West, the tradition of white holds when it comes to preparing the departed: no one would wrap a corpse in a black shroud. Thus, the mourners show respect for the dead by wearing black, while the deceased wears white in preparation for the afterlife.

MARRIED IN WHITE

Above: Widowed women
waiting to celebrate *Holi*
festival in northern India.

There is one perennial when it comes to white clothing: the wedding dress. In some parts of the world this tradition goes back to antiquity – in Ancient Greece, for example, brides wore white dresses, carried white flowers and painted themselves white. And a traditional bride in Japan wore a white kimono to symbolize the purity she would offer to her new home. White represents virginity in this respect, as a young bride was expected to be sexually untouched and naïve.

171

When we consider the long history of Western weddings, white is actually a relatively new style. Until the mid-nineteenth century, most women would wear their best dress for their wedding, whatever colour that happened to be, because they couldn't afford a new one.

These were outfits that could be worn again and again. Blue, grey, pearl, brown and even black were commonly chosen. White was an option but not a particularly popular one, partly because it showed stains more easily and was therefore less likely to last. In the Middle Ages, a bride's maids wore the same colour dresses as the bride because this was said to confuse the evil spirits, who might wish to harm the bride, so the choice of white would mean lots of irritated women tiptoeing through the wedding to avoid dirtying their dresses.

For the wealthy, and those from the aristocracy, the favoured colour was red. Royal brides tended to wear brocaded and embroidered gowns, often in the more expensive aristocratic red, but very seldom white. Mary Queen of Scots wore white to marry the French King Francis II in 1559, but when he died a year later, she was blamed for cursing him by her choice of a 'mourning' colour for her wedding.

Below: The bride and groom in a traditional Japanese wedding, the former wearing her white kimono.

Above: A medieval woman wears an expensive red dress for her wedding day, indicating her social standing (left); Queen Victoria's white wedding dress, which sparked the trend for pure white (left).

The European and American tradition of white weddings began with Queen Victoria who, on 10 February 1840, made what was considered a daring decision when she wed her German first cousin, Albert of Saxe-Coburg.

One reason Victoria chose white was to show off her handmade lace. The twenty-year-old petite queen arrived in her pure white, lacy gown, with white orange blossoms in her hair, and the public took note. The aristocracy felt obliged to go the way of the queen so they followed suit. Just nine years after Victoria's wedding the American publication, *Godey's Lady Book* rather overreached when it declared: 'Custom has decided, from the earliest ages, that white is the most fitting hue, whatever may be the material. It is an emblem of the purity and innocence of girlhood, and the unsullied heart she now yields to the chosen one.' Yet it took a while before white weddings became widespread, particularly for those not blessed with wealth. A much-cited nineteenth-century ditty dutifully puts white at the top, but offers several other acceptable alternatives.

Left: It was not until after Queen Victoria's reign that white wedding dresses became entrenched in the West.

Married in white, you will have chosen all right.
Married in grey, you will go far away.
Married in black, you will wish yourself back.
Married in red, you'll wish yourself dead.
Married in blue, you will always be true.
Married in pearl, you'll live in a whirl.
Married in green, ashamed to be seen,
Married in yellow, ashamed of the fellow.
Married in brown, you'll live out of town.
Married in pink, your spirits will sink.

By the end of the century white had taken over. The American publication, *Ladies Home Journal*, gave it the unjustified blessing of history: 'From time immemorial the bride's gown has been white.' Throughout Europe and America the popularity of white dipped during the First World War – a time of austerity – but it was revived after the war and has never looked back.

From about 1920 onwards, wearing a white wedding dress has been *de rigueur* for a first bride, particularly because it symbolized the virginity it was assumed the bride still possessed. Once that connotation became cemented, few new brides were bold enough to wear a colour suggesting otherwise. This association evaporated as the premium on virginity disappeared, but the popularity of the white bridal dress has hardly diminished. Still, there is some ambiguity these days about the sexual significance of white. For example, in modern France, where white wedding dresses remain popular, the term 'white wedding' nevertheless suggests one in name only – an administrative marriage of convenience.

WHITE, FLESH OR NUDE?

Paint specialists seldom talk of simple white. For them, white comes in a variety of shades that are bewildering to everyone else. We might all be familiar with eggshell, ivory and vanilla, but perhaps less so with ghost white, baby powder, white smoke, Dutch white, Navajo white, cornsilk, seashell, flax and Ecru.

But when it comes to skin colour, what is called white would be utterly perplexing for someone not familiar with racially stereotyped terminology. Even those suffering from albinism (lacking skin pigmentation) do not have 'pure white' skins. For the rest, 'white' skins might more accurately be described as peachy pink, florid pink, yellowish pink, olive, yellowish brown, beige, light brown, medium brown or cream with freckles, but never the white of milk or snow. So then, how did 'Caucasian' people (another misnomer, as the term doesn't always refer to skin tone) become known as 'white'?

WHITE DOVE REPRESENTATION
White is amply represented in both the Old and New Testaments of the Bible. For example, angels are said to wear white robes. So when it was said that the spirit of God was represented by a dove – for example, after Jesus was baptized by John the Baptist – it was naturally presumed this dove was white. However, none of the thirty mentions of doves in the Old and New Testaments say anything about their colour. In fact, white doves are not found in the wild and have only been bred by humans quite recently.

It all comes down to two things: colour associations and beauty ideals. As we've already seen, the connotations of white are largely positive – particularly in the West. It is the colour associated with purity, innocence, virginity and so on. So white already had a head start when it came to things that were desired, which brings us to beauty.

Until sunbathing took off, after the mid-twentieth century, the feminine ideal in Europe involved a skin that had little acquaintance with sunlight. Snow White was the fairest of them all, and descriptions of the beauties of previous centuries were inclined to dwell on their alabaster skins, the milky white of their breasts, etc. For most women there was no other option – their clothes covered their arms and legs and their bonnets shaded their faces. Those who worked in the fields, of course, found their

Left: The pale-skinned ideal of beauty in previous centuries.

faces and hands and perhaps their arms turned brown, and they were seen as rough and coarse – a long way from the ladylike ideal – their colour being indicative of a certain social standing.

So it was that white was valued – both because of the colour's cultural associations and because when it came to human skin, and particularly female skin, lightness was prized. It is hardly surprising therefore, that while brown-skinned slaves and colonial subjects from Africa were called 'black', their overseers and rulers called themselves 'white'.

However, the gap between depiction and reality created a problem. How do you describe the *real* colour of untanned European skin? That, of course, depends on which part of Europe you're talking about, but in English, the term 'flesh coloured' first emerged in the early seventeenth century to refer to a creamy pinkish, yellowish colour.

This took off in the twentieth century, when used to describe the colour of everything from children's dolls to women's underwear. Later in the century, however, the use of 'flesh' for a colour that resembled the flesh of no more than 10 per cent of humanity began to tail off. The word itself began to feel presumptuous and even offensive. For some, it was replaced with 'nude', which has precisely the same problems, suggesting that white people, who aren't really white, have nude skins, whereas black people, who aren't really black, do not have nude skins. The search for an acceptable and accurate colour for 'white' skin continues.

INUIT WORDS FOR SNOW

There's a story that goes round and round the internet: that the Inuit people have 200 words for snow, or is it 123 or sixty-seven or nineteen? The point of the tale is that because 'Eskimos' are always surrounded by snow they discern subtle distinctions in its whiteness and texture that the rest of us miss. The only problem is that it's not true. Their languages have the same number of words for snow as many others. More accurately, they use single terms, when other languages use terms such as powder snow, fresh snow or yellow snow.

THE PRICE OF BEAUTY

The idea that beauty required an alabaster white skin prompted the use of lead white paste as foundation, particularly in the eighteenth and nineteenth centuries. This paste was made from lead carbonate and, as even the ancients knew, lead white was highly poisonous. It was first produced in Anatolia, in the Asian part of Turkey, at least 4,300 years ago, and became a popular white base pigment for paints and cosmetics. Pliny the Elder warned that it was toxic, as did the Greek poet Nicander, who described it as a 'hateful brew'.

It was originally produced by placing lead shavings over a bowl of vinegar. The fumes would attack the lead and leave deposits of the white lead carbonate. In the seventeenth century, the Dutch invented a new method for producing it in large quantities, by using sheds to house huge clay pots divided in two – with vinegar in one half and the lead strips in the other. The sheds were then packed with cow and horse dung to warm them up and accelerate the chemical reaction, which took up to three months. Eventually, an unfortunate worker would be sent into the noxious environment to collect the lead white.

The warnings about the health implications kept coming. A seventeenth-century report by the Dutch artist Philipbert Vernatti, told of the symptoms experienced by the workers who collected the lead strips: acute fevers, shortness of breath, dizziness, 'great pain in the brows', blindness, loss of appetite, 'frequent vomitings', 'paralytic affections' and 'stupidity' among others. In effect, they were being poisoned to death.

Its first recorded use as a cosmetic goes back to Greece, in the fourth century BC and to Ancient China in the same period. Face-cream made from lead white became particularly popular in Europe and the United States in the eighteenth and nineteenth centuries among well-heeled society women, who used it to give their complexions the desired alabaster look. It duly killed many.

One of these was the celebrated Irish Countess, Maria Gunning, known both for her beauty and her vanity. She became so addicted to the stuff that it caused skin eruptions, prompting her to use more and more of it (to cover up the flaws) until she could no longer bear to show herself in public. She suffered

Right: Maria Gunning, who became addicted to the white face paint she used.

from a number of ailments, including chronic constipation, and eventually was said to have gone insane before dying from lead poisoning, at the age of twenty-seven, in 1760. In high society circles at the time, it was said she was a 'victim of cosmetics'.

Yet this awareness of its toxicity had minimal impact. More than a century after Gunning's death, the US cosmetics company, George W. Laird, was still running magazine advertisements for its popular 'Bloom of Youth' foundation, which was made mainly from lead white. Other lead-based cosmetics came with names like 'Ali Ahmed's Treasure of the Desert' and 'Eugenie's Favourite'. By the end of the nineteenth century new synthetic cosmetics replaced lead white, but lead white was only banned in the United States in 1977.

The country where it did most harm was Japan, where it was widely used by Geisha women, the wives of Samurai warriors, courtesans, actresses and by women in the upper classes during the three centuries of Shogun rule.

Japanese researchers recently studied the bones of Samurai children and found that they contained levels of lead fifty times higher than normal. The cause was found to be the white facial powder (made from lead white and mercury chloride) used by the women, who would inadvertently poison their children through breast-feeding.

This caused a range of ailments, including brain damage, and may have contributed to the demise of Shogun rule by 1868. As one of the researchers noted: 'A ruling class afflicted with brain damage isn't a recipe for success.'

WHITE WITH FRIGHT

The main reason one's hair changes colour over time is genetics, which is why identical twins tend to go grey in tandem. Yet there are many stories of people's hair suddenly turning white. Marie Antoinette was said to have gone white overnight, shortly before she reached the guillotine. Curiously there are no cases of modern death-row prisoners abruptly changing hair colour and the reason is that hair can't change colour spontaneously. For that to happen, thousands of coloured hairs would need to fall out and thousands of colourless (white) ones would need to sprout overnight.

It is certainly true that some people's hair can turn white relatively quickly, however, if not overnight. Stress and illness can have this aging effect on hair, so it is possible for someone's hair to go white if they experience a shock or trauma of some kind.

Those who claim they are going grey with stress are therefore not wrong, but nor are they completely right. This is because grey hair is really an optical illusion. A hair either has its original pigment or it has turned white. There is no middle road. It is the *combination* of hairs of your original colour and white hairs that give the impression of grey. The popular perception is that, as we age, our hair gradually changes colour, becoming dark grey, then lighter grey and eventually white. In fact, hairs simply stop producing pigment one by one. As we approach middle age, the cells in the follicles of new hairs start to die, which means they cease producing pigment. So while the hair continues to grow it arrives devoid of colour – white. This absence of pigment is called achromotrichia.

WHY IS THE WHITE HOUSE WHITE?

Simply because people in the eighteenth century had a passion for everything Grecian and they mistakenly believed that Greek marble sculptures and buildings were white. They therefore faithfully reproduced what they thought was the style of the Ancients – from their columns to their white marble buildings and sculptures. Many years later when techniques were found to analyse the composition of surfaces, it was discovered that the Ancient Greeks were fans of garish colour, and painted everything in bright hues. Over the centuries the paint weathered and wore off, prompting this neo-classical error.

Right: A nuclear bomber, painted white in order to deflect some of the thermal radiation of nuclear blasts.

WHITE NUCLEAR BOMBERS

When materials are heated they turn from red to yellow to white. Nuclear explosions give off a blinding flash of white heat, which prompted the US Air Force to paint their nuclear bombers white, which really does help to deflect some of the thermal radiation of the white flash of the nuclear explosion. This brilliant white became known as 'anti-flash white' and continues to be used on US, British and Russian nuclear bombers.

BLACK

THE MAIN ASSOCIATION OF BLACK IS, of course, darkness – the complete absence of light. This element of the unknown stirs the imagination and is part of the mystery associated with black. In most cultures, black is also associated with death. Certainly it is integral to Western death-related symbolism – a colour of coffins, of mourning clothes and undertakers' suits and the Black Mariah hearse. This is also part of its meaning in India and much of Africa, and in many other parts of the world. For example, the Ndembu people of the Congo draw a black line from the navel to the pelvis on the corpse of a person who died without descendants – a sign that they have died forever. The Ancient Egyptians viewed black as the colour of the grave, and the god Anubis was portrayed as a black-headed jackal (see previous page). They called their country 'the Black Land' because of their beliefs about the darkness that preceded creation and the fertility of the lands around the Nile. The black-clad Nyx was the Greek goddess of the night, who was there at the start of creation and mothered other deities, including Hypnos (Sleep) and Thanatos (Death), and in the day she is associated with the mysterious Furies and the Fates.

EVIL BLACK

When one associates black with death, unfathomable mystery, the dark unknown and the deepest night, it is not much of a leap to associate it with magic, evil and plain bad luck. In the Western tradition there is black magic and the black arts, black Masses and black Sabbaths. Black cats are associated with witchcraft and misfortune, and black dogs have been variously associated with death, evil and depression. The villains in early Western movies wore black hats and black clothes. In Christian symbolism black has long been the colour of Satan, his fallen angels and hell.

Again, this association crosses continents and cultures – black, darkness, magic, sin, evil. Through much of Africa it is associated with sorcery. For example, some Hausa people, of Nigeria, fear the dangerous black gods, who drive people mad, paralyse them and strike them dead. They call a sad person a 'black belly' while one described as having a 'black heart' could be angry, or dishonest, or any kind of enemy – a term also used in some Arab countries to refer to anyone considered overly vulgar.

Ghanaian Kente cloth weavers use bands of black, which were once said to represent original sin, but also represent intensified spiritual energy. In Ancient India, black was used to depict evil and terror, and a range of other negative traits. In imperial Japan, about a thousand years ago, wearing black signified carrying bad fortune, which was why those who wished to absent themselves from society – monks and recluses – wore black. Today a Japanese person might use two words, *hara guroi*, which translates as 'black stomach', but metaphorically means 'wicked'. In parts of modern Indonesia black is the colour of demons and of disaster, illness and left-handed people. This has to do with their use of one hand to eat and the other to perform ablutions, for the sake of hygiene and avoiding illness, a practice also found in India.

Below: Nyx, Greek goddess of the night (left), and the terrifying black form of the Indian goddess Kali (right), who stands for both destruction and life-giving, and is here worshipped by the great gods Indra, Brahma, Vishnu and Shiva.

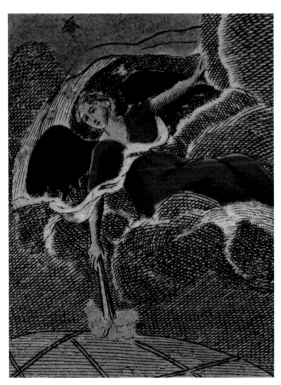

In some parts of the world black has acquired uniquely negative connotations. In Sweden and Norway black is the colour of jealousy and envy – instead of going green with envy, they go *svartsjuk*, which means 'black-sick' – and in Finland, those consumed with jealousy are said to have it *mustasukkainen*, which means 'with black socks'.

STRENGTH IN BLACK

Black is not always regarded negatively. One view of black is similar to the idea of vaccination – the thing that causes evil can also protect one from evil. The original reason why Indian parents used black kohl as eyeliner for their children was to protect them from evil spirits. In some parts of India there was a custom of adding a pinch of charcoal to milk, because of the belief that white could attract evil, and black could protect against it.

In other parts of the world, black had more ambiguous and sometimes even positive meanings. The first Chinese emperor, Win Shi Huange, 2,300 years ago, chose black for his colour, because it was said that 'black water quenches red flames' – a reference to his overthrow of the red Zhou dynasty.

In Chinese colour symbolism, black variously represents water (as seen down a well), the direction north (represented by the black tortoise), the planet Mercury, winter, cold, the pig, the chestnut, millet and a dormant state of development. Black also represents the 'full yin' – the opposite, dark force to the light force of yang, which is represented by white.

For several Native American tribes, black was associated with masculinity, with power, aggression and strength, and was used as face paint for war – charcoal mixed with animal fat or saliva. In some of the drier parts of the world, black is the colour of fertility, representing rich soil. For example, in parts of north-west Africa, women wear black dresses after a week of marriage, to symbolize fertility and reflect transformation – the symbolism drawn from the colour of rich soil.

PIOUS BLACK

In the Western tradition, the colour of death also became the colour of penance, which is the reason why one sees black bunting in Catholic churches during Lent. From this root, it became one of the colours of the Church and, particularly, of churchmen. Cardinals might wear red and bishops purple, but the clergy and nuns wore black from the sixth century AD, although at least until the late Middle Ages the lack of black dyes meant that it was actually a dull, dark grey.

The dull black problem was partially remedied – at least for those with money to spend – in the late fourteenth century, when the means to create deeper, darker blacks were found through triple-dyeing (dyeing blue, yellow and red together produced a

The Inquisitor General, Tomás de Torquemada (centre), in his black robes.

lasting and dark-enough black) and this new, richer black became the colour of the perpetrators of the Inquisition. The Spanish priests tasked by the Pope with the mission of burning and torturing to ensure purity of faith, arrived in their ominous deep black robes. This same principle of mixing colours to achieve black is still used in black inks, for felt-tip pens and so on.

The new wave of religious fundamentalists, who emerged from the early sixteenth century – Calvinists, Lutherans, Protestants, Anglicans and their offshoots – embraced this tradition, which fitted with the severity and austerity of their heaven and hell beliefs.

Black had become associated with modesty and piety and seriousness and was therefore seen as the appropriate colour for Puritans. They viewed black robes as suitable dress, not just for ministers but for their congregants too – a sober, sombre colour for modest, humble, God-fearing people. This was aided by laws that made black the obligatory colour for mourning all over Europe during the sixteenth and seventeenth centuries.

Below: Martin Luther (left) and John Calvin (right) both favoured black as a symbol of their faith.

PIRATES, PURITANS AND BLACK GOLD

The sumptuary laws that prevailed for several centuries throughout Europe enforced strict limits on who could wear which colours. Black fell outside these strictures, which is one reason why its popularity grew. By the seventeenth century almost all of the professions of the rising middle classes had adopted black for their work wear – bankers, lawyers, judges, merchants, doctors. It showed seriousness of purpose, honesty, piety and professionalism.

One of the problems was that, unless one was prepared to pay a high price, one still had to make do with a black dye drawn from oak galls – made by gall wasp larvae on oak branches – and this had the habit of fading to a dull, dark orange colour fairly quickly.

Other options included using blackberries and walnuts, and these delivered a dye that was better than the oak-gall black but was still more like a dark grey. Or one could use iron filings soaked in vinegar, but this too produced a dark, dirty grey colour.

The best alternative to pricey triple dying was first to dip the cloth in woad to create a blue base, and then to use a particular bark called logwood to lock in the black. But these logwood trees were found only in the crocodile- and mosquito-infested

THE BLACK-SWAN CONUNDRUM

There's an old adage frequently used for factually unlikely claims: absence of evidence is not evidence of absence. The black swan is one of the examples used to demonstrate this line of argument. Until about 200 years ago, no one in Europe had seen or heard of black swans. There was no evidence of black swans, so was this evidence of the non-existence of black swans? In reality, black swans were thriving in Australia and New Zealand, and would soon be imported. In other words, the absence of evidence of black swans turned out to be evidence of nothing more than inadequate information.

mangrove swamps of Spanish Central America, which created a problem for the English in particular, because imports of logwood made big profits for Spain, so the English rulers banned it in 1581.

In 1673 the ban was lifted after peace was negotiated between the English and Spanish empires, which led to England gaining a small and uncertain foothold in Central America – the former British Honduras, which is now Belize.

Enter the pirates. For more than a century, brigands had been doing brisk business by relieving Spanish ships of the booty they had plundered from their colonies. While the Spanish remained England's great rivals, the latter turned a blind eye to their exploits, but once peace arrived, the Crown no longer tolerated piracy so the privateers had to find other ways of making their living.

Many retreated to British Honduras and got into the now legal logwood black dye business on what became known as the Mosquito Coast. So the clothes of the Puritans were dyed using logwood imported by pirates forced to change their careers.

BLACK POWER, BLACK PRIDE

No race is 'black' in the literal sense – and those defined that way, or who define themselves that way, have skin colours ranging from very light brown to very dark brown. So why is it that all shades of brown skin are labelled 'black'?

Like so many things, this goes back to slavery. The men, women and children who survived the slave ships came mainly from West Africa, where skin colour is typically dark brown. Just as the pink or cream-coloured slave-owners called themselves white, so they called their slaves black, or words derived from black – 'negro' comes from the Latin *niger*, which means black.

Some slave-owners routinely raped their female slaves, producing mixed-race offspring, adding to their 'stock'. The United States abolished slavery in 1865, but the slaves and their mixed-

Above: A slave ship arrives in Virginia with slaves for sale.

race descendants remained in the same 'black' category, and laws discriminating against them, particularly in the southern states, did not distinguish between shades of skin tone. Thus, anyone who was of either African descent or mixed-race identified with the same racial group – now black, but originally coloured.

Several political groups campaigned to forge a positive black identity, and in the 1960s the 'Black Power' movement emerged, asserting a more militant black consciousness, seen in the stands taken by sports stars – particularly Muhammad Ali, who was stripped of his world title after refusing to be drafted into the US military. As he put it, 'They [the Viet Cong] never called me "n*****".'

In 1968 two African American athletes, Tommie Smith and John Carlos, raised their black-gloved fists while 'The Star-Spangled Banner' played at the Mexico City Olympics, after winning the 200-metre gold and bronze medals respectively. They both wore black socks (and no shoes) and Smith also wore a black scarf as a symbol of black pride. Afterwards, he said: 'If I win, I am American, not a black American. But if I did something bad, then they would say I am a negro. We are black and we are proud of being black. Black America will understand what we did tonight.'

This specifically black identity has since been promoted through slogans like 'Black is Beautiful' and assertions of black pride, through Black History Weeks in high schools and most recently through the Black Lives Matter campaigns. And it spread internationally, most notably to apartheid South Africa where in the late 1960s the Black Consciousness movement came to the fore under young leaders like Steve Biko. He saw it as a way of combating inherited notions of black inferiority because, as he put it, 'The most potent weapon in the hands of the oppressor is the mind of the oppressed.' His definition of 'black' included anyone who had been oppressed by apartheid and therefore covered not just the African majority but also mixed-race people and those of Indian descent. Biko said that being black was 'not a matter of pigmentation: being black is a reflection of a mental attitude'. He was murdered by the apartheid security police in 1977. Eventually the apartheid regime fell and Nelson Mandela came to power as the first black president of South Africa.

Left: Tommie Smith (centre) and John Carlos (right) raise their arms in the Black Power salute at the 1968 Olympic Games in Mexico City.

HOW DID THE OLYMPIC MOVEMENT RESPOND TO THE BLACK POWER SALUTE?

In 1936 the Nazi-praising president of the US Olympic Committee, Avery Brundage, supported athletes giving the Sieg Heil salute during the Berlin Olympics. He went on to become the President of the International Olympic Committee and in this capacity was outraged when Tommie Smith and John Carlos made a black protest salute at the 1968 games, which he said was inappropriate for the 'apolitical' Olympics.

This was different from Berlin 1936, he insisted, because, unlike the Black Power salute, the Nazi salute was a 'national salute'. He ordered Smith and Carlos to be banned from the Olympic village and threatened to ban the entire US track team if this didn't happen.

The result was the expulsion of the two medallists. They and their families later received death threats. Australia's silver medallist Peter Norman vocally supported Smith and Carlos and joined them in wearing an Olympic Project for Human Rights (OPHR) badge on the podium. The OPHR had called for the removal of 'Slavery Avery' from his post.

Norman was cautioned by Australian Olympic bosses and was not picked for the 1972 Munich Olympics, where two black American 400-metre medallists – Vincent Matthews and Wayne Collett – also protested on the podium, and were also banned. The IOC (International Olympic Committee) eventually made quiet peace with its past, posting on its website in 2013: 'Over and above winning medals, the black Americans athletes made names for themselves by an act of racial protest.'

THE LITTLE BLACK DRESS

Until the twentieth century the main use of black in Western clothing was to show temperance, modesty and mourning. And it retains these roles, which is part of the reason why it remains a favoured colour for men's suits, shoes and evening dress, and why, for many years, it was the prime colour of cars, phones, bicycles, Bibles and the like – things to be taken seriously. For most of his life, the ostensibly pious Henry Ford refused to allow any other colour for his cars – his mythical catchphrase was 'You can have any colour, as long as it's black.'

But from the second decade of the twentieth century it emerged as a multi-faceted colour of fashion that went way beyond the desire to show sobriety and serious intent. This started with what became known as the little black dress or LBD, which first emerged as a cocktail frock in the late 1920s, with Gabrielle 'Coco' Chanel being among its earlier designers and champions. As she put it: 'Women think of all colours except the absence of colour. I have said that black has it all. White too. Their beauty is absolute. It is the perfect harmony.'

From the start, the LBD was relatively short, straight and uncomplicated although its length rose and fell a bit according to the morés and fashions of the day. In the 1940s and 1950s it came to suggest a risqué element – that of the 'loose' and dangerous woman.

Its aficionados included Edith Piaf and Wallis Simpson. In the 1960s it emerged in miniskirt form as an element of youth culture, but it also acquired a touch of sophistication, with Audrey Hepburn in her Hubert de Givenchy-designed LBD in *Breakfast at Tiffany's*, seen as the epitome of a certain kind of femininity. Today it remains as popular as ever, viewed as a timeless perennial for any woman with a regard for fashion. As Christian Dior would have it: 'You can wear black at any time. You can wear it at any age. You may wear it for almost any occasion; a "little black frock" is essential to a woman's wardrobe.'

Trendy black is not restricted to ladylike Hepburn-wannabes in their LBDs. Combined with combat boots (usually black) it became a favoured colour of grunge culture in the 1990s, and an essential for Goths and Berlin trend-setters.

Aside from dresses, black is a much-favoured option for jeans, T-shirts, blouses, skirts, scarves, hats, coats, nail polish, you name it. Wednesday Friday Addams, the fictional Addams Family character, wouldn't think of wearing anything else. 'I'll stop wearing black when they make a darker colour,' she said.

Anyone wanting to look a bit thinner, or more sophisticated, or a bit more sullen or sombre, or a bit dark, deep and mysterious, or wanting to highlight their pale complexion, would reach for black. In the right hands it retained its signature of rebellion.

Johnny Cash was also an appreciator of black's appeal: 'I wore black because I liked it. I still do and wearing it still means something to me. It's still my symbol of rebellion – against a stagnant status quo, against our hypocritical houses of God, against people whose minds are closed to others' ideas.'

WHY WAS THE BLACK DEATH BLACK?

Bubonic plague was called the 'black death' because it left dark patches under the skin, caused by subcutaneous bleeding, then parts of the body would die and turn black – necrosis. By the time victims died, they were often black and disfigured. Although we now know that the disease was carried by black rats and spread by fleas, this was not understood at the time.

The earliest European references to the 'Black Death' go back to 1350, such as Belgian astronomer Simon de Cevino's reference to the *mors nigra*, but it took until 1823 to acquire that name in England. There were repeated outbreaks until early in the eighteenth century in Europe, the mid-nineteenth century in the Ottoman Empire and China and the early twentieth century in pockets of Australia and America, by which time it might have killed as many as 200 million people worldwide. The last outbreak was reported in Madagascar in 2014.

Other terms have been used for different outbreaks, such as

The Great Mortality or Death, and The Great Plague. There is some uncertainty about whether it was the same disease each time. Also, the black death pathogen comes in three variants – bubonic, pneumonic and septicaemic plague.

Below: An illustration depicting a couple suffering from the blisters of the bubonic plague that swept through Europe in the Middle Ages.

BLACKING UP

For many years black film and theatre roles were given to white actors, who 'blacked up' with boot polish or paint. Some of the most famous, or infamous, included Al Jolson in *The Jazz Singer* (the first-ever movie with sound, made in 1929) and Laurence Olivier in *Othello* (1965).

Actors like Olivier 'blacked up' because theatre hadn't thought of finding black actors to play the Shakespearian hero, or anyone else for that matter. But the objection was not just from giving the very few black roles to white actors; it also related to history. What is known as 'blackface' goes back to the American minstrel shows that started in the slavery era.

Below: Laurence Olivier blacking up to play the role of Othello.

White actors would paint their skins black to portray either the 'dandified darky' or the 'happy-go-lucky plantation worker'. These shows continued in the United States until the early 1960s when the Civil Rights Movement drove them out of town, and they kept going in the UK until the 1978, when the BBC's *The Black and White Minstrel Show* came to an end after a twenty-one-year run. Quite remarkably the black comedian, Lenny Henry, appeared in the show in 1975. He later explained that he had been contractually bound and wasn't in a position to object.

BLACK FRIDAY

Ever since 1952 the day after American Thanksgiving has been viewed as the start of the Christmas shopping season, which means most big stores stay open at night and many offer bargains. Shoppers respond accordingly. But why 'Black'? Some have claimed it is because the shops' balance sheets go into the black numbers (profit) or even that the skies are always dark at that time of the year.

The real reason is that, for many years, bad days were dubbed 'black' (the financial panic of 1869 was first dubbed 'Black Friday') and for shop assistants and the police, this is a bad day because of the ensuing stress and chaos.

The first use of the term came in its first year, in Philadelphia in 1952, by police who despaired at the crowds and congestion, and the resulting mayhem that often included traffic accidents and violence. By the mid-1970s the term had become widely used. This tradition, and the name Black Friday, spread to Canada and Mexico, then all over Europe, and to India, South Africa, New Zealand, Colombia and several other countries.

ΘΥ ЄΡΗΝΗ

ΗЄΥ
СЄ
ΒЄ
ΤΛΗ

GOLD

IT'S THE PRIZE FOUND AT THE END OF THE RAINBOW, the well-spring of wonder, delight and riches. It gives its name to anything that strives towards perfection. Whenever triumph is rewarded, it is part of the accolade – the gold-coated medals given to the winners of races, or the gold-plated statues given to the men and women who star in winning films. Whatever we are said to value, silence included, gets gilded.

Like silver, gold is not strictly a colour (though it snuggles up to yellow), but today it is very much part of the colour spectrum – an option for ostentatious or ironic decoration for anything from robber-baron limousines to gold lamé dresses.

Once, gold paint came from expensive and very tricky gold leaf, but no longer. These days various synthetic versions are available for anything requiring ostentation, whether kitsch or faux-kitsch. For those who want to make their own it is easy enough to blend – by mixing a little bit of brown with a lot of lemon yellow and a touch of white, although an artist, looking for an accurate depiction of gold, would instead try to paint the colours reflected in the gold object.

The most renowned gold painting is certainly Gustav Klimt's *Portrait of Adele Bloch-Bauer I* – a 1907 portrait of his wealthy Viennese patron and friend, Adele Bloch-Bauer. This painting, which portrays Bloch-Bauer in a sumptuous, swirling dress in shades of gold, with a vivid gold background, was the last work in what was later called his 'golden phase', painted over three years with oils as well as gold leaf. It was seized by the Nazis from the Bloch-Bauer home in 1941 and displayed without any reference to the fact that it portrayed a Jewish woman (calling it simply, 'Portrait of a woman'). In 2000 Bloch-Bauer's niece, Maria Altmann, sued Austria for the return of the portrait in American courts, which she eventually won, prompting the 2015 film *Woman in Gold*, starring Helen Mirren.

When we are talking about gold it is hard to separate the colour from the substance – the impact of the former comes from the value of the latter. Ever since it was first mined, or panned, and used for artefacts in the Middle East (probably more than 7,000 years ago), gold has taken its place at the apex of all the metals.

Its relative rarity, its lustre, its malleability as a soft metal and its resistance to tarnishing, have given it a remarkably consistent versatility, both in its ornamental form in jewellery and other displays of wealth and opulence and as currency. In the twentieth century it found added uses as an electronics connector, a photographic toner, a false-tooth cover, a reflective layer on up-market CDs, a Formula 1 heat shielding and as an ultra-thin de-icing layer for aircraft cockpit windows.

KING MIDAS AND THE GOLDEN TOUCH

Gold's value comes at a cost, as societies, ancient and modern, have long recognized, giving rise to several cautionary parables about the moral cost of the greedy quest for gold that have resonated through the ages.

Perhaps the most resonant is the story of King Midas and his deathly golden touch. The real Midas ruled Phrygia, in Greece, in the seventh or eighth century BC. After his death (said to have been suicide from drinking bull's blood) a number of legends arose, including the one that anything he touched would turn to gold.

In this early Aristotelian version, he starved to death after his 'vain prayer' was granted. The Roman poet Ovid picked up on this. In his version the god of the harvest, Dionysus, found that his own foster father and teacher, the satyr Silenius, was missing. Silenius was found by peasants and carried to King Midas, who recognized him and gave him the full royal treatment, before returning him to Dionysus.

The grateful god then offered Midas a wish, and he chose the golden touch. However, when his food, drink and everything else turned to gold, he cursed his prayer. Bits and pieces were added to the story over the centuries and, in the nineteenth-century version, recounted in a children's book by the American novelist Nathaniel Hawthorne, Midas's beloved daughter is added. He touches her, and she too turns to gold, after which he pleads to Dionysus, begging for delivery from starvation. He is told to wash in the river Pactolus, and he is delivered from the golden curse as the river turns to gold. Midas came to hate gold, and hate wealth, and instead turned to worship the god of wild nature, Pan.

The allegory behind this legend has been a literary perennial. Take, for instance, the oft-repeated phrase, 'all that glitters is not gold', which suggests that not everything that looks valuable or precious or delightful turns out to be quite so wonderful. This was the opening line of one of the riddles posed, in 1596, by the Shakespearian heroine Portia in *The Merchant of Venice*, and it goes on to warn that 'Gilded tombs do worms enfold'. Neither Portia nor Shakespeare claim originality. After all, the second line of Portia's riddle is 'Often have you heard that told'.

Right: King Midas's golden touch turns his daughter to gold, a salutary lesson to all those who covet wealth and riches.

· MIDAS' DAUGHTER · TURNED · TO · GOLD ·

An earlier telling is found in Chaucer's *Yeoman's Tale* – 'But al thing which that shyneth as gold / Nis nat gold, as that I have herd it told'. Chaucer stuck to this theme in *The House of Fame* – 'Hyt is not al golde that glareth'. Like the Midas legend, this one goes back to the ancients: the Latin phrase *Non omne quod nitet aurum est* translates as 'All that glisters is not gold'.

A (relatively) modern variant, which inverts the Midas theme, comes from George Eliot's magnificent allegorical novel *Silas Marner*, in which the eponymous hero lives an isolated, soulless life, accumulating gold, but when this is stolen from him, he finds, instead, an orphaned baby girl, the golden-haired Eppie, and raises her as his own daughter, finding happiness and contentment, which spreads to all those he touches.

GOLDEN SECRETS

Discoveries of gold change people and countries. When gold was found in Coloma, California in 1848, 300,000 people flocked to the state over the following year to seek their fortunes and San Francisco was transformed from village to city. They became known as the 49ers.

Most gold is found in rocks under the earth's surface, and much of this comes from mines in southern Africa. It was the source of one of the last great wars of the nineteenth century, or the first of the twentieth, the Anglo-Boer war of 1899–1902, when the British relieved the Boers of the land they, in turn, had taken from the Africans. The gold rush of the Witwatersrand, which began in 1886 and led to the development of Johannesburg, came about 900 years after the first gold miners in the region made their discoveries.

In 1935 archaeologists, appointed by the South African government, discovered an Iron Age site on a hill called Mapungubwe, near the Limpopo river. Objects found there, dating from AD 1000, included ornaments made from glass, tin, ivory and copper, as well as pottery. And there were also several objects made from gold, which were used as burial gifts for the elite.

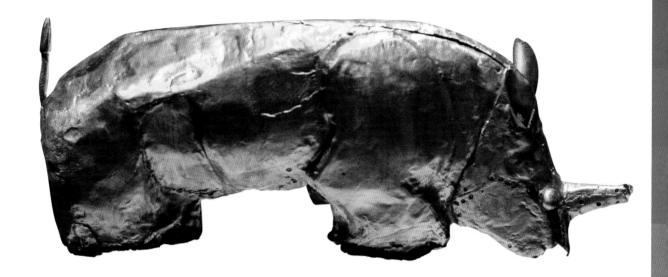

The gold-leaf covered rhino from the hilltop settlement of Mapungubwe, South Africa.

The most striking is a small, intricately carved rhino covered in gold leaf, made in the thirteenth century. The gold was mined and smelted in the local area during that time. The white government officials protected this site and kept the findings secret, because they were not keen for it to be widely known that African people were gold miners and sophisticated goldsmiths hundreds of years before Europeans set foot in the area. Many of these objects were found in a locked room in Pretoria, eight years after the country became a democracy.

It is now known that Mapungubwe was part of a network of fortified Iron Age trading centres, linking the gold-rich mines in southern Africa along the east coast of Africa, stretching all the way to what is now Tanzania, with trading connections that reached to China, India and the Middle East.

The most impressive of these city-states is what is now known as Great Zimbabwe, a 722-hectare royal palace that housed 18,000 people. Its construction began 900 years ago and it is now estimated that about 20 million ounces of gold were mined around Great Zimbabwe in the 200 years after it was constructed.

Accounts from fifteenth-century Portuguese traders described it as being surrounded by gold mines. The white Rhodesian government banned its archaeologists from telling the truth about it (that it was built by the predecessors of the Shona people from the eleventh century) and instead were told to say it was built by Arab 'Hamite' people at an unknown date.

THE COLOUR BLONDE

Attractive young women with fair hair are periodically referred to as 'golden-haired beauties', although anyone with hair that was really the colour of gold would look rather odd. Another option is 'yellow' but aside from the folk singer Donovan – 'Yellow is the colour of my true love's hair' – there weren't many takers for yellow as an adjective for women's tresses. So instead, we have a word with more pizazz than fair, and less ostentation than golden: blonde (or blond for men, and as an adjective for both).

The hair colour itself, which comes from the low levels of the dark pigment, eumelanin, sometimes takes on an additional adjective – white-blond, golden-blond, honey-blond, platinum-blond, strawberry-blond, sandy-blond, dark-blond, ash-blond, dirty-blond and, of course, golden-blond.

Above: The ruins of the city-state of Great Zimbabwe, one of the centres of gold mining in Africa.

The first English reference to blond hair goes back to 1481, but it took a long time to eclipse 'fair'. Its origins are French, which in turn inherited it from Medieval Latin, which used *blundus*, a bastardization of the Ancient Latin *flavus*, which really does mean yellow.

Nowadays, 'blonde' has taken on all sorts of meanings of its own. A man might be described as having blond hair, but he's seldom 'a blond', yet for a woman this hair colour might be taken to define her very existence: 'She's a blonde' or 'She's that tall blonde over there' or 'She's become a bottle-blonde'.

Again, there are adjectives to go with it – for example, a 'ravishing blonde' might also be a 'dumb blonde' who might be asked, 'Are you having blonde moment?' On a more assertive note, the pop star Madonna's provocatively raunchy 1990 world tour was called 'Blond Ambition', which might have in some way inspired the book and 2007 film *Blonde Ambition* (about a smart blonde who eventually wins success).

It might look otherwise in public, but 98 per cent of the world's population do not have naturally blond hair. And yet some evolutionary psychologists argue that blond hair evolved through sexual selection – that through some undefined biological process in male brains, men evolved to find blond hair inherently sexy.

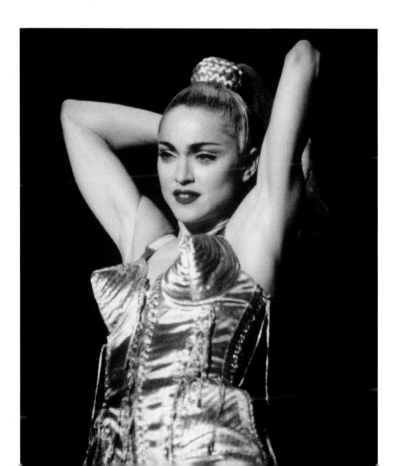

Right: Madonna's 'Blond Ambition' world tour was a more assertive use of the 'blonde' label.

However, there is no evidence for this view and the geographical patterns of prevalence indicate a purely environmental origin.

Blond hair first evolved in Scandinavia and the Baltic Sea countries, where it is most prevalent today – more so than in Germany, where the Nazis saw blond hair as being part of the Aryan ideal. Its evolution relates to natural selection for lighter skin in more northerly countries because lighter skin synthesizes vitamin D using sunlight's UV rays better.

However, if one's ancestors lived in a part of the world nearer one of the poles, but had a diet high in seafood and certain other proteins, there would have been less evolutionary need for lighter skin and hair, which is one reason why the Inuit have black hair and darkish skins. Recent genetic research conducted at three Japanese universities isolated the genetic mutation for blondness and dated its occurrence to about 11,000 years ago.

Blond hair is no more innately attractive than brown, black or red. And its current cultural status wasn't always quite so secure. After all, when the Brothers Grimm wrote *Snow White* in 1812, they gave their heroine hair 'as black as coal'. The increasing appeal of blond hair was enhanced by its visibility in

Left: Marilyn Monroe's blond locks have been credited with the colour's enduring popularity in the twentieth century, as well as its association with sex appeal.

early monochrome films, and from there to the models chosen for advertising campaigns, and back again.

Ever since the heyday of Marilyn Monroe in the 1950s, it has been associated with sex appeal, which might be the reason why some surveys suggest that blond waitresses get the biggest tips.

It has also long had an intrinsically youthful impact because children born with blond hair often find it turns brown as they get older. But modern hair dyes have democratized blondness by making it more accessible, leading many darker-haired women to conclude that if blondes really do have more fun, and gentlemen really do prefer blondes, well then, why ever not?

In the 1950s just 8 per cent of British and American women over the age of twenty-five coloured their hair. Today, according to studies in both countries, the figure is variously said to be between 50 and 75 per cent, and the colour of choice is one or another shade of blond. Growing numbers of men seem to be following suit, including from those countries with very few natural blondes. Will they too come to be called dumb blonds – or golden-haired beauties?

WHEN DID SILENCE BECOME GOLDEN?

The phrase that implies that keeping quiet is better than speaking your mind has rather obscure origins. The English poet and novelist, Thomas Carlyle, borrowed it from Swiss-German and translated it in his 1836 novel *Sartor Resartus*, which has much to say on the subject of silence. He writes, 'As the Swiss Inscription says: *Sprecfien ist silbern, Schweigen ist gold* (Speech is silver, Silence is golden) …' This, in turn, is said to go back to AD 600 when the phrase was used in a Jewish rabbinical commentary called the 'Midrash', which contains numerous homilies. Perhaps the best use of the phrase came from Muhammad Ali who said: 'Silence is golden when you can't think of a good answer.'

AFTERWORD

Almost from the moment of birth we are bombarded with disparate colour-based facts and opinions.

No matter which culture we are born into, we are given basic information about most of the primary and secondary colours, depending on the beliefs and customs of that culture. The meanings of some colours, of course, are widespread: red is associated with blood and danger, among other things; white always has at least one of its connotations as purity.

Yet even when it comes to the definitions of colours, what one learns might depend on time and place. Once one moves beyond defining colours and naming things associated with them, and enters the world of symbolism, the associations become harder to pin down.

For at least 100,000 years modern human beings, with brains like ours, have lived lives rich with symbolism. It is a significant part of what makes us human – our ability to imagine, to think in the abstract, to put ourselves in someone else's shoes and to use language to communicate our thoughts, desires and dreams. Colour is a significant part of this. It helps us to ascribe meaning and status to the bewildering world we encounter.

But our choice of symbols is less universal than we might think, for the simple reason that different environments, different histories and different cultural experiences prompt disparate ways of viewing the world and of imagining other people's lives. So it is hardly surprising that the meanings of colours wax and wane and change over time, and from place to place.

Sometimes, these alternative meanings go deep into the pores of a culture. We can only guess why black became associated with death in some parts of the world, and not others. At other times, culturally based meanings come from very specific sources. The English-speaking world sees envy as green because of the writing of their greatest playwright and poet more than 400 years ago. The Islamic world gives exalted meaning to the same colour because of key figures from the Qur'an.

But no matter whether the sources are ancient or modern, most of us absorb our colour concepts from the earliest of days and develop set ideas about what different colours mean, and even about what is right and wrong when it comes to colour choice. We might assume that our way of seeing colours is universal although, in reality, most of these are inherited ideas, and inheritance can change over time. In other words, our perception of colour, and of different colours, is culturally contingent.

What this book has tried to show is that once we get beyond the most elemental meanings of a colour – blood, fire, purity, death, life – the rest of the colour spectrum is up for grabs.

ACKNOWLEDGEMENTS

Without the help of several people, this book would never have happened. I would like to thank two in particular: my energetic agent, Andrew Lownie, who has represented me for my last three books and negotiated this one, and my ever-encouraging editor, George Maudsley, who fed me with ideas, always responded to mine, and steered it through to the end, including the editing and picture approval. He was always a pleasure to work with. Also Judith Palmer, whose picture research has made this book the thing of beauty it is, and designer Darren Jordan for his sterling work in putting the pieces of this puzzle together.

BIBLIOGRAPHY

Research for *The Story of Colour* started with a series of interviews and discussions with artists and other experts in the use of colour. It also involved reading numerous academic papers in obscure journals relating to colour and colour perception. And, of course, it involved extensive internet research. It also drew inspiration from previous books relating to colour, particularly the following, all strongly recommended:

Johann Eckstut and Arielle Eckstut, *The Secret Language of Color*, Black Dog and Leventhal Publishers, New York, 2013.

Victoria Finlay, *Colour*, Hodder and Stoughton, London, 2002.

Victoria Finlay, *The Brilliant History of Color in Art*, Getty Publications, Los Angeles, 2014.

David Hornung, *Colour: a workshop for artists and designers*, Laurence King Publishing, London, 2012.

Derek Jarman, *Chroma*, Century, London, 1994.

Kassia St Clair, *The Secret Lives of Colour*, John Murray, London, 2016.

Jude Stewart, *Roy G Biv: An Exceedingly Surprising Book About Color*, Bloomsbury, New York and London, 2013.

Anne Varichon, *Colours: What They Mean and How to Make Them*, Abrams, New York, 2006.

PICTURE CREDITS

Page 81
Editorial cartoon, 1899

Page 83
Mary Evans Picture Library

Page 85
Vincent Van Gogh, *The Good Samaritan (after Delacroix)*, 1890, Kroeller-Mueller Museum, Netherlands; image The Yorck Project: *10,000 Meisterwerke der Malerei*, DIRECTMEDIA Publishing GmbH

Page 86
Moviestore Collection/REX/Shutterstock

Page 87
Illustration of The Yellow Kid by Richard Fenton Outcault reprinted from *Antique Phonograph Monthly* magazine, vol.3, no. 8 (Oct. 1975) courtesy of Allen Koenigsberg (publisher) and Robert Feinstein (author)

GREEN
Page 88–9
Asif Waseem/Shutterstock.com

Page 91
Thoom/Shutterstock.com

Page 93
(left) Illustration by Arthur Rackham from *A Midsummer-Night's Dream* by William Shakespeare, Doubleday, Page & Co., New York (1914)
(right) Buyenlarge/SuperStock

Page 95
© The British Library Board. All rights reserved./Bridgeman Images

Page 97
Illustration from *Robin Hood and his Merry Outlaws*, George Harrap (c. 1910); image © Look and Learn

Page 98
Transcendental Graphics/Getty Images

Page 100
Anna Pakutina/Shutterstock.com

Page 101
Arthur Simoes/Shutterstock.com

Page 102
Michael Pacher, *St. Augustine and the Devil*, c. 1471–75, Alte Pinakothek, Munich; image The Yorck Project: *10,000 Meisterwerke der Malerei*, DIRECTMEDIA Publishing GmbH

Page 103
Esa Hiltula/age fotostock/SuperStock

Page 104
Fine Art Images/SuperStock

Page 107
Illustration by Arthur Rackham from *Peter Pan in Kensington Gardens* by J. M. Barrie, Hodder & Stoughton, London (c. 1912)

BLUE
Page 108–9
Kokhanchikov/Shutterstock.com

Page 111
(left) Werner Forman/Universal Images Group/Getty Images
(right) Werner Forman/Universal Images Group/Getty Images

Page 112
(top left) BBC Motion Picture Gallery/Getty Images
(top right) BBC Motion Picture Gallery/Getty Images
(bottom) paveir/Shutterstock.com

Page 115
Courtesy of YouGov/yougov.com

Page 116
(left) age fotostock/SuperStock
(right) ACME Imagery/SuperStock

Page 117
(top) © Ashmolean Museum/Mary Evans Picture Library
(bottom) Ephotocorp/age fotostock/SuperStock

Page 119
(left) Jaroslav Moravcik/Shutterstock.com
(right) Durham Cathedral Library, MS A.I.19A, folio 207v, reproduced by kind permission of the Chapter of Durham Cathedral

Page 120
Jon Super/AFP/Getty Images

Page 122
Leonid Andronov/iStock

Page 123
Mehmet Cetin/Shutterstock.com

Page 125
Illustration by Gordon Frederick Browne from *Heroes & Heroines of English History* by Ernest Nister (c.1895); image © Look and Learn

Page 126
Quick Shot/Shutterstock.com

Page 127
Education Images/UIG via Getty Images

Page 129
Illustration from *Il Costume Antico e Moderno*, vol. I, by Giulio Ferrario, Florence (1826)

Page 131
Courtesy of the Advertising Archives

Page 133
Courtesy of the Advertising Archives

PURPLE
Page 134–5
age fotostock/SuperStock

Page 137
Mosaic of Emperor Justinian I, Basilica of San Vitale, Ravenna; image The Yorck Project: *10,000 Meisterwerke der Malerei*, DIRECTMEDIA Publishing GmbH

Page 139
Illustration from *Antony and Cleopatra* by William Shakespeare, Booklovers Edition, The University Society, New York (1901)

Page 141
Illustration by Warwick Goble from *The Complete Poetical Works of Geoffrey Chaucer*, The Macmillan Company, New York (1912)

Page 142
valeaielli/iStock

Page 143
akg-images/Pictures From History

Page 145
Science and Society/SuperStock

Page 147
From the 1922 Standard Color Card, Fall Season, issued by the Textile Color Card Association (now CAUS)

Page 148
Henry Diltz/Corbis via Getty Images

Page 151
Yawar Nazir/Getty Images

PINK
Page 152–3
Courtesy of Patrick Carney of thepinktriangle.com

Page 155
Photo by Manfred Brueckels/Wikimedia Commons/CC BY-SA 3.0

Page 157
(left) Thomas Gainsborough, *Francis Nicholls 'The Pink Boy'*, 1782, oil on canvas; 1676 x 1168 mm; Waddesdon (National Trust) Bequest of James de Rothschild, 1957. acc. no. 2508. Photo © National Trust, Waddesdon Manor (right) Jacques-Emile Blanche, *Portrait of a boy in a pink sailor suit*, 19th c./Private Collection/Roy Miles Fine Paintings/Bridgeman Images

Page 158
George Karger/Pix Inc./The LIFE Images Collection/Getty Images

Page 159
Courtesy of Historyworld.co.uk

Page 161
(top left) Courtesy of The Advertising Archives
(top right) Courtesy of The Advertising Archives
(bottom) 1955 Dodge La Femme advertisement

Page 162
(top) Courtesy of The Advertising Archives
(bottom left) 1969 Lustre Creme advertisement
(bottom right) 1968 Lustre Creme advertisement

Page 164
John Moore/Getty Images

WHITE
Page 166–7
Zurijeta/iStock